An Idio
Guide
to the
Bible

by
Derek Williams

© Text Derek Williams
© Maps, illustrations, bookmark, time-line charts and appendices Peter Kaye

ISBN 1-85078-447-7

Published in 2002 by Paternoster Lifestyle

Paternoster Lifestyle is an imprint of Paternoster Publishing,
PO Box 300, Carlisle, Cumbria, CA3 0QS, UK
and Box 1047, Waynesboro, GA 30830-2047, USA

08 07 06 05 04 03 02   7 6 5 4 3 2 1

British Library Cataloguing-in-Publication Data
A catalogue record for this book is available from the British Library

Typeset by Land & Unwin (Data Sciences) Ltd
Bugbrooke, Northamptonshire
Printed by Bell & Bain Ltd., Glasgow

CONTENTS

The New Testament

PREFACE

This book is an attempt to simplify the Bible and make it easier to understand.

I have wanted to try and produce a simple guide to the Bible ever since I became a Christian in 1983. This book began to take shape in my mind after a friend called Elaine said to me 'You have to write the book you can't find in the library'. I decided it needed an authority to help write it. I shared my ideas with Derek Williams and his first response was to describe the suggested style as 'rather Procrustean' – a word I had to look up in the dictionary.

It turns out that Procrustes was a robber in a Greek myth, who put travellers in his bed and stretched or lopped off their limbs so they fitted it. So Procrustean means producing conformity by violent means, and Derek applied it to my idea of giving every book in the Bible the same amount of space. I could see his point, but I persisted in asking him to write the book in this form, believing that the violent conformity might at least bring a bit of simple clarity.

I am very grateful to Karen Kaye for all her help with drawing the maps. The maps are intentionally diagrammatic. They are designed to make a simple point, and are not meant to be geographically precise or exactly to scale.

I would like to thank Martin Steele and Tim Whitaker for reading through the manuscript and for their helpful comments. I am also grateful to Hillary Austin for her expert typesetting.

Peter Kaye
Editor

INTRODUCTION

The Bible was the first book to be printed and it remains the world's best selling book. It sells over 45 million copies a year, and parts of the Bible have been translated into over 2000 different languages – a lot more than its nearest rivals (60 translations for Shakespeare, 120 for the Koran).

The Bible remains the most bought book, but it is not the most *read* book. Many people admit to finding it difficult to read.

This short book is designed to provide a brief overview of the Bible without having to balance a Bible, a Bible commentary and a Bible map on your lap all at the same time. It is written for all those well-meaning people who don't read their Bible enough – which is most of us!

It is generally well known that the Bible is in 2 parts, the Old Testament (full of blood and thunder and warfare) and the New Testament (about a perfect man called Jesus Christ). It is less well known that the Bible is also written at 2 levels. It is a story based in historical fact, but at a deeper level it is about the inner spiritual journey of each of us. It is a mirror that reflects our innermost selves.

The BIG question for us is not just 'What does the Bible mean?' but 'What does the Bible mean to me?'. We are intended to read it with a view to applying it, because it tells us how to live:

> *All Scripture is God-breathed*
> *and is useful for teaching,*
> *rebuking, correcting and training*
> *in righteousness,*
> *so that the man of God*
> *may be thoroughly equipped*
> *for every good work.*
> 2 Timothy 3.16

So why do we need to study the Bible? Because what it means now depends on what it meant then. The Bible cannot suddenly mean what it never meant.

This little book is meant to encourage you to read the Bible every day – as a way to happiness. Taking in the Bible every day (like 'daily bread'), and living by it, leads to happiness (blessing):

> *Blessed is the man*
> *who does not walk*
> *in the counsel of the wicked*
> *or stand in the way of sinners*
> *or sit in the seat of mockers.*
> *But his delight is in the law of the Lord,*
> *and on his law he meditates*
> *day and night.*
> *He is like a tree planted by streams of water,*
> *which yields its fruit in season*
> *and whose leaf does not whither.*
> *Whatever he does prospers.*
>
> Psalm 1

THE BIBLE STORY IN BRIEF

•**In the beginning** God created a perfect world, then he created man, then it all went wrong (but it wasn't his fault). The rest of the Bible is about how he tried to put it right again.

•**Adam and Eve** spoiled the perfect Garden of Eden by giving in to temptation (the snake was offering good food and inside information). Things got worse, so God decided to wash his hands of the whole affair and ordered a flood. But he saved Noah (and a zoo) so he didn't have to start completely from scratch. But success was short-lived (Noah got drunk) and the people started fighting, so God started again with Abraham.

•**Abraham**, a nomad, was called by God to become the father of a great nation. Abraham seemed an unlikely choice, because he was old and infertile, but miracles do happen and he became a dad at a hundred. His great-grandchildren ended up in Egypt, and *their* great-grandchildren were forced into slavery.

•**Moses** (the 'Spartacus' of the Old Testament) rescued them, after clobbering Egypt with a series of plagues. But they had to spend 40 years wandering in the wilderness before entering the 'promised land' of Canaan (Palestine) because they complained so much about the desert menu. Moses passed his time in the desert climbing a mountain to fetch the 10 commandments, writing out laws and building a worship tent.

•**His sidekick Joshua** led the assault on Canaan. When the walls of Jericho collapsed the country was their oyster. The 12 tribes of Israel spread out, and were mercifully spared central government by their itinerant judges, who settled arguments and sometimes doubled as military generals. But the Israelites kept forgetting God, which landed them in trouble.

•**They asked for, and got a king** (Saul) who turned out to be a manic depressive. He almost murdered his successor, David, who united the tribes (and made Jerusalem the capital) and brought peace. God's promise seemed to be coming true. David's son Solomon presided over a golden age of prosperity. But surprise surprise, that didn't last either. After Solomon's death there was a BIG Argument.

•**The nation split** into two: Israel in the north and Judah in the south. The Bible follows the fading fortunes of both, concurrently.

•**Prophets like Elijah and Isaiah** (God's messengers) kept poking their noses in and warning the kings to mind God's business, or they would be punished. But the kings just kept telling the prophets to mind their own business – until the story begins to sound like a scratched record, playing the same old tune. The prophets finally proved correct. The people were taken captive by nearby empires and carried away into exile.

•**Israel** went through 19 kings (none of them any good in God's sight) and was eventually destroyed as a nation by the Assyrians.

•**Judah** struggled on for another 120 years, getting a few good kings among the 20 who tried to rule it (good kings like Asa, Jehoshaphat, Hezekiah and Josiah). Eventually the nation of Judah (with Jerusalem as its capital) was crushed by the Babylonians, who gave the cream of the people a one-way ticket to see Nebuchadnezzar's hanging gardens.

•**The exile in Babylon** lasted around 70 years. Whilst in Babylon Esther rescued them from annihilation, and prophets like Daniel and Ezekiel tried to keep them on the right track. Then Cyrus the Persian took control of Babylonia and declared a general amnesty for political prisoners. Many grateful Jews returned home to Jerusalem to start again.

•**They rebuilt the temple** (under the watchful eye of prophets Haggai and Zechariah), and later re-instated the law (under the critical eye of Ezra) and rebuilt the city walls (under the authoritarian eye of the inspirational Nehemiah). Nevertheless they remained at the mercy of the Persian Empire, and awaited the great Messiah that the prophets had foretold.

•**For the next 400 years** the prophets were silent, during the Greek and Roman rule. The tribe of Judah eventually became the Roman province of Judea – which gave the Jews their name. By 4 BC, under Roman occupation, people were expecting and longing for their Messiah to come and rescue them, but only a few shepherds and foreign astrologers noticed his arrival.

•**John the Baptist** emerged 30 years later, and cried in the wilderness 'to prepare ye the way of the Lord', and Jesus Christ leaped into the limelight.

4

• **Christ** was famed as a teacher and as a healer. He chose 12 men to be his apostles and 70 other helpers to spread his message. People came to think of him as the Messiah, but he was so different from the Messiah the people expected that eventually he was arrested for blasphemy, went through a mockery of a trial, was sentenced to be crucified by an indifferent Roman governor (Pontius Pilate) and nailed to a cross between 2 thieves.

• **Christ rose from the dead,** 3 days later. His demoralised disciples couldn't believe their eyes when they saw him alive again, but after some persuasion and an influx of the Holy Spirit they set about turning the world upside down (or right way up, depending on your viewpoint) with the Christian message.

• **Within 30 years churches were spreading** (groups of people, not buildings) from Judea to Spain (aided by the excellent roads and single language of the Roman Empire). For their efforts some of the early Christians were jailed and others killed. The star turn was Paul, who saw the light on the Damascus road and became the foremost evangelist and theologian. The emperor Nero crucified both St Paul and St Peter (with whom Paul did not always see eye to eye) but the church carried on regardless.

• **The last of the apostles,** John, hung on until near the end of the first century, writing the book of Revelation from a prison camp on the Greek island of Patmos to sustain his persecuted friends. And the rest is history.

SUMMARY OF THE SUMMARY

- **Genesis**   The creation, and the fall into sin
- **Old Testament**   God chooses a nation to bring his revelation of Himself
- **Gospels**   God reveals Himself, in the person Christ
- **Acts/Letters**   The early church
- **Revelation**   How the world will look once evil is overcome

THE OLD TESTAMENT

GENESIS 1-11

Overview

'Genesis' means 'beginnings'. Genesis 1-11 is the prologue, about the beginning of the world, the beginning of man and the beginning of sin (sin being rejection of God). In the beginning God created the world. There was darkness and chaos, and then God brought light and order – a picture of our own internal struggle. Next God made sky, earth, sea, sun, moon, stars, fish, birds, animals and finally man. God made man in his own image, so we must have God-like characteristics within us (the

---

TOP PERSONALITY – ADAM

Adam's name means 'man'. Adam was given the job of looking after God's world but fluffed it when he got greedy. Which makes him what the Bible says he is, representative of the rest of humanity. Adam took the forbidden fruit then hid from God, but God found him out. Adam blamed Eve and Eve blamed the serpent, and people have been blaming each other ever since.

---

problem being to locate them). Then, on the seventh day God rested. The fact that rest is necessary, even for God, must be the most overlooked idea in Western Civilization. The other main stories are about Adam and Eve, Cain and Abel (the first murder), Noah and the flood and the Tower of Babel. Simple stories telling of a good and fair God who caused the world to happen and made human beings special (*all* of them, not just your friends).

However the people fought against the rules and lost their place in Eden, which was God's tangible presence. God and the people drift apart and have a few angry exchanges (like the Flood). The rest of the Bible is about how they get together again.

Link to Christ

Christ is seen in the New Testament as 'the second Adam'. Adam got us in a twist by telling God to get lost, and ended up getting lost himself. Christ obeyed God, and so Christ can straighten us out – if we ask him.

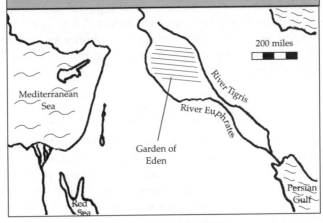

TIME AND PLACE
This is pre-history – the time of the New Stone Age when cultivation, culture, and communities got a kick start from somewhere (or Someone). The Garden of Eden is said to be in Mesopotamia in the fertile crescent between the 2 great rivers, known to be the cradle of civilisation, and now the playground of Saddam Hussein.

200 miles

Mediterranean
Sea

River Tigris

River Euphrates

Garden of
Eden

Persian
Gulf

Red
Sea

THE GARDEN OF EDEN

So what's the message?

You may have grown out of believing that you were found under a gooseberry bush; you may believe you evolved from The Primeval Slime. But that doesn't tell you WHY you exist. Genesis does. Genesis says you (and *everyone* else) matter personally to God. Whatever your mother may have told you, you are not An Accident. God made a world system for us to live in peacefully, on one condition: that we didn't turn our backs on him. God made YOU, so read his operating manual, which explains how to be truly human. Then thank God for making you.

Key verse

> *So God created human beings in his own image, in the image of God he created them; male and female he created them.*
>
> Genesis 1:27

9

GENESIS 12-50 – THE PATRIARCHS

Overview

Now the action begins. This is an everyday story of country folk. Folk like doddery Abraham who became a dad when he's 100, his son Isaac, his grandson Jacob who was a liar and a cheat, and pompous Joseph, dreaming his dreams and strutting his designer jacket. They have no schools, factories, computers, cars, microwaves, TVs, phones or flushing toilets. After all, they're only a few generations beyond the garden of Eden. But they *do* have religion.

TOP PERSONALITY – ABRAHAM

Abraham is still revered by both Jews and Muslims, and saluted by Christians when they bother to read the Old Testament. Abraham's great strength was blind faith in God: he did what God said without always understanding why. 'Faith' to Abraham simply meant 'trust in God' – which is the working definition of "faith" used by the rest of the Bible.

It's a primitive religion, though, because the Bible isn't yet written. Stories and beliefs were passed down orally, and developed phenomenally accurate memories. So they were discovering God as they went along, often making mistakes.

The people you meet here are called 'Patriarchs' – our spiritual fore-fathers. They eventually started the twelve tribes of Israel. They were singled out by God to be his pupils and to show his purposes to the world.

Link to Christ

Abraham's faith is used by St Paul, in his New Testament writings, as an example of how we should believe in Christ. Then as now, people reckoned that to get back to God, you had to earn your passage. Abraham was different. He just trusted what God was doing. Paul says, do the same with Christ – trust him and trust what God's doing through him.

So what's the message?

Let's be honest. Do you really think God's got any use for all the mistakes

ABRAHAM'S JOURNEY AND JOSEPH'S TRIP TO EGYPT

you've made in life so far? Especially those big ones you'd rather weren't headlined in a Sunday tabloid. In fact you'd be wrong.

Take Abraham. He had a bit on the side, with the connivance of his wife, who then got jealous. Then there's young Jacob, who cheated himself to the top, then fled to a foreign tax haven. Or spoiled-brat Joseph who got up his brothers' noses so much, they bought him a one-way ticket to hell on earth, as a slave in Egypt. If you haven't guessed, it all ended happily ever after (more or less). And the point is that God was involved in it all, like a craftsman weaving together damaged threads to restore a tapestry to its intended beauty – like Joseph's coat of many colours. If he could make use of these guys, there's hope for you yet.

Key verse

'You intended to harm me, but God intended it for good to accomplish what is now being done, to the saving of many lives. So then, dont be afraid.'
Joseph, speaking to his brothers: Genesis 50:20,21

11

EXODUS

Overview

Genesis ended with corn in Egypt. Exodus opens 400 years later – and the fortunes of the Hebrews have changed. They are slaves of a surly Pharaoh (= 'Fuhrer') who pre-dates Hitler and oppresses the Israelites. Exodus means 'leading out' and is about Moses rescuing his people by leading them out of slavery in Egypt.

After years of unanswered prayers God comes to the rescue. He gets Moses' mother to hide him in a waterproof basket in the bulrushes, just near to where the royal family go swimming, Moses is saved from the latest round of infanticide, and God arranges for him to be brought up as

---

TOP PERSONALITY – MOSES

Moses was a hero. Slave emancipator, Prime Minister, Commander in Chief, Lord Chief Justice (he put God's laws together in a form the Israelites could understand) and Lay Chairman of General Synod (he sorted their church out). Above all, he was truly a man of God. Moses spent 40 years being a "somebody" (an Egyptian prince) 40 years being a "nobody" (an exile in hiding) then 40 years being a "somebody for God".

---

a prince. But the young prince murders a stranger and goes on the run for 40 years.

Eventually, Moses meets God in a fresh way (at a burning bush), and goes back with his brother Aaron to Egypt and leads the Israelites to freedom (after 10 plagues convince Pharaoh that God's trying to say something). Once out, they spent 40 years in the desert during which God gave them the ten commandments (see Appendix 3, page 147).

Relation to Christ

The 'Exodus' is about rescuing God's people from slavery, and is a picture of Christ's rescue of people from their slavery to the bad ways of the world. The 'law' of Moses was a major issue when Christ came on the scene. Christ said he came to fulfil it, (which most people thought meant 'to abolish it').

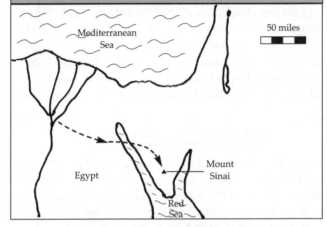

Mediterranean
Sea

50 miles

Egypt

Mount
Sinai

Red
Sea

THE ROUTE OF THE EXODUS

So what's the message?

The 10 plagues finally changed Pharoah's mind. The plagues were natural occurrences spread over 9 months. Nile floods brought red silt down the river, producing blood-red colour, foul taste, dead fish and fleeing frogs. Gnats and flies bred in warm damp conditions, and spread diseases (animal anthrax and human skin conditions). Unusual weather conditions brought giant hailstones, locusts breeding fast and feeding faster, followed by sandstorms, borne on the regular Hamsin winds.

All in a day's work for God, and not a natural law out of place. So here we see him as the Lord of creation who uses natural events as vehicles for his message.

Key verse

Who among the gods is like you, O Lord? Who is like you – majestic in holiness, awesome in glory, working wonders?

Exodus 15:11

LEVITICUS

Overview

I grew up downwind from a whelk stall on Ramsgate sea front. The thought of picking salt and vinegar flavoured lumps of gristle out of glorified snail shells, to say nothing of swallowing slithery jellied eels, does nothing for me. (Well, it does, but I'd better not say what.)

If you've got a food fad, then you're halfway to understanding Leviticus (which few people ever read). It's all about clean and unclean foods, clean and unclean personal discharges, all mixed in with some bloody sacrifices. It's pretty picky about sex, too, and who you can or can't have it with. Leviticus 23 describes the main Jewish festivals (see Appendix 4).

TOP PERSONALITY – AARON

Aaron was Moses' kid brother. He was the first high priest and the book of Leviticus describes the rituals he had to perform. He acted as Moses' spokesman (Moses was very shy, and had a stammer). The book of Exodus describes how once, when Moses was off talking to God, Aaron caved in to public opinion and made the people a bull-calf idol to worship. We all make mistakes, but that one deserved impeachment.

The book of Leviticus was a handbook for the Levites (the priests). On the surface, these are religious fads you either like or don't. But under the surface it was the Israelites' way of learning about God in a practical and very physical way.

Link to Christ

The New Testament letter to the Hebrews goes to town on Leviticus (so no-one ever reads the letter to the Hebrews, either). The book of Hebrews draws a parallel between the rituals of Leviticus and the death of Christ. Christ did permanently what the rituals could only do temporarily – bring God's forgiveness to people like you and me.

So what's the message?

The laws and rituals in the book of Leviticus point to *truths* which are still valid, even if the rituals themselves are not. For example, they stress that

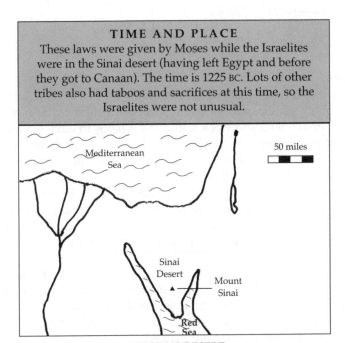

THE SINAI DESERT

God's people are to be different to others in their reasons for living and consequent lifestyle together.

The Israelites are called to be 'holy' meaning 'set apart for God's use'. (That's why pots and pans can be described in the Bible as 'holy', meaning set apart for use in rituals). The rituals were a visual aid to the rest of society that a social order based on faith in God was both possible and effective. In the early church, the Christians amazed some onlookers by their generous love. They put community care into action.

The laws and rituals also remind us that God is interested in the details of life. There is nothing that cannot be 'sacred', because there is nothing that is merely 'secular'. God made everything, after all.

Key verse

I am the Lord your God. Consecrate yourselves and be holy, because I am holy.

Leviticus 11:44

NUMBERS

Overview

The book of Numbers gets its name from a census, when God's people were counted up. Despite its name, you don't need to be nimble with figures to understand this book (although it helps to have nimble fingers to skip over chapters 1-4, 7 and 26 which are archives from the government statistics office, and chapters 5, 15, and 28-30 which are extracts from the priests' training manual).

The rest of Numbers is about their wanderings in the desert. God kept them going in circles till they learned to stop moaning. It contains some

---

TOP PERSONALITY – BALAAM

It ought to be Moses, but we've had him, so let's give Balaam his 15 minutes of fame. He was a pagan prophet summoned by Balak, king of Moab, to curse the Israelites before they got into the promised land. But each time Balaam opened his mouth, God's words of blessing poured out instead. Balaam lost his agreed fee, but he went home a wiser man.

---

entertaining stories. You might have problems with the one about Balaam, which takes us into Dr Dolittle's realm with a talking donkey. It reminds Christians that God can 'speak' in all sorts of funny ways, and that everything around us can speak to us of God.

Link to Christ

A plague of poisonous snakes invaded the Israelite campsite, interpreted as God's punishment for the people's disobedience. Moses made a bronze snake icon to represent God's justice. Those who looked at it were healed. In the same way, John's Gospel says, people who look up to Christ on the cross will receive God's new start.

So what's the message?

'Numbers' ought to be called 'warnings' – it's all about the Israelites doing what they shouldn't and reaping the consequences. Even Moses got it in the neck. It took a short time to get the Israelites out of Egypt but a long time to get Egypt out of the Israelites.

The people moaned a lot. When they moaned about the unreliable

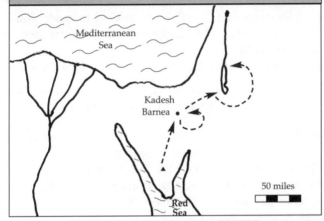

TIME AND PLACE
Numbers is the story of the Israelites' semi-nomadic
meanderings in the semi-desert of Sinai (they were a bit
semi-detached from God, too). They spent 40 years on a
journey that could have taken 11 days. The date is 1270 –
1230 BC (between exiting Egypt and entering Canaan).
The desert was scrubland more than sand dunes.

Mediterranean
Sea

Kadesh
Barnea

50 miles

WANDERING IN THE SINAI DESERT

water supply, God showed Moses a new aquifer. But instead of turning
the tap on with a prayer as he was told, he belted the rock with his stick as
if he had some magic power. For that silly trick, he did a forfeit. He died
before his people could enter the promised land of Canaan.

Then there was Korah, who led an abortive coup against Moses, but
overlooked the fact that he'd pitched his tent on the thin crust covering a
deep bog. His clumsy bid for leadership came to a premature end when
he put his foot through the floor and sank into oblivion.

The author is saying you might not see God, but he can see you. So
don't think he's missing your tricks. He may be loving, but he's not stupid.

Key verse

The Lord said to Moses, 'How long will these people treat me with
contempt? How long will they refuse to believe in me, in spite of all the
miraculous signs I have performed among them?'
Numbers 14:11

DEUTERONOMY

Overview
Deuteronomy explains God's *covenant* with the Israelites. (It had to happen sometime – a theological word: 'Covenant.') If you give to charities you'll know about 'deeds of covenant', when the tax you paid on your gift goes back to the charity. Basically, a covenant is an agreement, with conditions.

The agreement was this: 'I will be your God to guide you – and you will be my special people.' The small print was less attractive: 'So long as you keep my commands.'

This book repeats quite a lot of the laws, but it is more about God's

---

TOP PERSONALITY – MOSES

After all he's been through, Moses deserves a second term at the top. He gets a superb obituary from an unknown hand in this book. There was no-one like him, it says, because he knew God 'face to face'. He was already 80 years old when he started his 40-year contract working for God, making more recent elder statesmen pale into insignificance.

---

loving patience in keeping his side of the bargain. It shows that God is caring and understands human weakness. If you think the God of Moses is different to the God of Jesus, read Deuteronomy, which proves he is not.

Link to Christ
Quiz time: What's the greatest commandment? Jesus said it was 'Love God, and love your neighbour as yourself.' And where did he get that from? Deuteronomy, of course! It was all there in black and white long before Jesus drew attention to it. Jesus also used other quotes from this book to beat off the devil's advances, during his 40 days in the desert.

So what does it all mean?
You know those rare people you come across who seem warm and wise and kind and just plain good to be with? Well, that's how God is portrayed here. Sure, there's some rules and regulations that seem a bit odd (even nice people have their funny ways), but God gave the laws because he loves them and wants the best for them – and us.

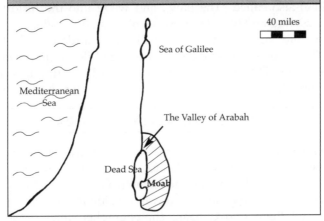

TIME AND PLACE

Moses wrote Deuteronomy whilst still in the desert (1290-1230 BC). 600 years later king Josiah rediscovered this 'Book of the law' and led a national revival based on it. Scholars reckon it was probably edited into its present form in David or Solomon's time (about 1000 BC).

THE PLACE WHERE MOSES SPOKE, JUST BEFORE THEY ENTERED THE PROMISED LAND

So dip into it and enjoy the feelings. 'I didn't choose you because you were stronger than other tribes,' God tells the Israelites, 'but just because I loved you.' Isn't that nice? He feels the same about us, too.

Or this, 'When you get rich, don't forget where you came from and what God did for you.' But we do, of course. Which is why the book's loaded with warnings, too. You can't expect God to keep his promises for ever if you don't keep yours.

Key verse

> *Know therefore that the Lord your God is God; he is the faithful God, keeping his covenant love to a thousand generations of those who love him and keep his commands. But those who hate him he will repay to their face with destruction.*
>
> Deuteronomy 6:9,10

JOSHUA

Overview

Now the tempo changes. We've left the 'Pentateuch' (the first five books of the Bible) also called 'The Law', and we're into the history section. Before it was thud and blunder; now it's blood and thunder.

The Israelites mass on the east of the river Jordan, ready to invade Canaan. There's one problem: the river is in full flood (it's spring; wrong time of year for D-Day landings). In a miracle of timing a landslide upstream lets them cross. They win the battle of Jericho (when the city

---

TOP PERSONALITY – JOSHUA

Joshua was Moses' sidekick in the desert. He was one of 12 spies sent by Moses into Canaan. Joshua produced a minority report saying they could beat the locals, with God's help, but no-one believed him. So they all had to wait outside for 40 years. Joshua finally led them into Canaan, choreographed their battles and organised their civil government.

---

walls fall down after a silent march of witness) and march on. After some stirring battles the Israelites parcel the land out among the 12 tribes of Israel (derived from the 12 sons of Jacob). They've arrived, in style.

Link to Christ

The names Joshua and Jesus both mean 'God saves' but the similarity seems to end there, because Joshua saved by killing God's enemies and Christ saved by being killed. But in fact their missions were similar, even if their methods were different: to bring people into the place God had prepared for them.

So what's the message?

Here's a band of ex-slaves following a God they still don't know too well trying to establish their identity in a society of warring tribes. So what does God do? Tell them to lay down their arms while he preaches the Sermon on the Mount? They're not ready for that yet. They couldn't understand it or begin to apply it. (It's hard enough for us.)

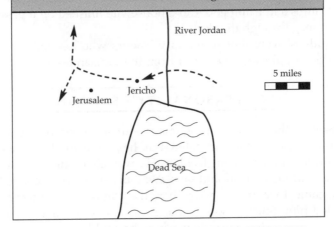

THE ISRAELITES CROSS INTO THE PROMISED LAND

So God starts where they are and leads them slowly towards a better way, using the methods of the time. (There's a brilliant encounter between Joshua and an angel in which God says he's not on any army's side, but that if Joshua follows God then he'll get what he wants.)

Where was God at earlier points in *your* life, when you knew even less about him than you do now? He was where you were, prodding you forward to where you are now. Sometimes we have to step into difficult situations to experience God's help.

Key verse

'As I was with Moses, so I will be with you; I will never leave you nor forsake you. Be strong and courageous.'
God speaking to Joshua. Joshua 1:5,6

JUDGES

Overview

This is the really juicy part of the Bible, and reads like the tabloids, with Samson's exploits sinking to the level of headlines such as 'Freddie Starr ate my hamster'. For example, Samson trapped 300 foxes, lit their tails and then set them loose to burn all the Philistine crops. Gideon beat an army with 300 lamps and trumpets. And a housewife finished off a passing king with a tent peg through the skull.

The 'judges' were mostly military leaders who rescued the Israelites from various oppressors (Deborah from the Canaanites, Gideon from the

---

TOP PERSONALITY – SAMSON

Samson is the Bible's strong man with a zipper problem. His marriage wasn't consummated but he made up for it with a prostitute and then with Delilah. He was also a bit slow, letting Delilah cut his hair off and take away his strength. A comic hero who came to a tragic end when the Philistines captured and blinded him. But Samson gets as much space in the book as the serious leaders. If God could use him, he could use anyone.

Midianites, Jephthah from the Ammonites and Samson from the Philistines). The serious point to the stories is that every Israelite generation forgot the lessons of the past. They turned away from God and 'everyone did what was right in his own eyes' and as a result they became oppressed. But each time they got round to asking for God's help, he sent a 'judge' to save them. The same thing happens in our own lives: forgetting God in good times, calling for help in bad times.

Link to Christ

The judges were 'saviours' who repeatedly rescued their people from God's judgement (judgement in the form of brutal tribes who rape, pillage and harass the Israelites). In the New Testament, Christ also rescues his people from their just deserts, after they have pushed God to the sidelines.

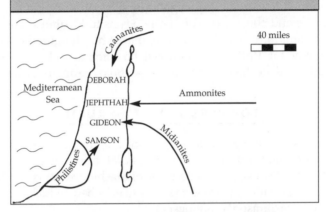

JUDGES FIGHT OFF SURROUNDING ENEMIES

So what's the message?
In a moral universe we can't escape for ever the consequences of our
actions (and attitudes) even though it often seems we have.

The author of Judges is making that one simple point. The Israelites
ignore or reject God (or try to marry him to incompatible religious
practices), and eventually they suffer for it. When we play God, the world
starts to fall apart because we lack that certain something that he's got.

The good news is that God doesn't give up on us so easily.

Key verse

*Again the Israelites did evil in the eyes of the Lord, so the Lord
delivered them into the hands of the Philistines for forty years.*

Judges 13:1

RUTH

Overview

From the tabloid revelations of Judges we move straight to the women's magazine tear-jerker of Ruth. It's a love story – but don't despise it; it's superbly written, well-constructed, and very moving. And it's a true story. Naomi, a Jew, moves to neighbouring Moab during a famine. Her husband dies and she marries off her two sons to Moabites. The sons die too, and Naomi returns to Israel. Ruth, one of her daughters-in-law, goes with her. Not for Ruth the traditional hostility to in-laws. Then Boaz meets Ruth, and he takes a second look. Boaz happens to be Naomi's

---

TOP PERSONALITY – RUTH

Ruth was charming, attractive, gentle, loving, devout, patient, hard-working, loyal, stoical in grief, and all round just plain good to be with. However, the book is the old fashioned Mills and Boon type and doesn't say what she was like in bed (which makes a change from Samson's conquests.)

---

relative, and so he has the right (and in Israelite law, the duty) to marry Ruth. He does, and they live happily ever after. (Which, despite what the tabloids say, does happen sometimes.)

Link to Christ

Ruth was King David's granny, and therefore a direct ancestor of Christ. The book of Ruth reminds us that Christ was descended from a foreigner. This was very significant to later Hebrew minds because Christ's worldwide mission was to both Jews and Gentiles (See Family Line – inside back cover).

So what's the message?

Ruth introduces us to the concept of 'salvation'. The Hebrews had a rule that when a woman was widowed and childless (like Ruth) the nearest relative had to marry her (even if he was married already) and make babies to keep the family line going. Boaz was the lucky fellow. He is called 'kinsman redeemer'; he 'redeems' the family line and brings hope and new life. Christ is called 'redeemer' in the New Testament, because he

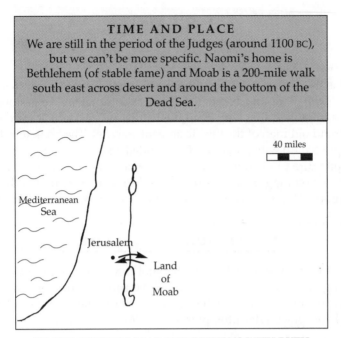

40 miles

Mediterranean
Sea

Jerusalem

Land
of
Moab

NAOMI GOES TO MOAB AND RETURNS WITH RUTH

too redeems God's people and brings them hope and new life. It's a
classic example of how big theological ideas were expressed in ordinary
people's experience. When Christ died and rose, people could look back
and say, that's like what Boaz did for Ruth.

Key verse

*Ruth replied, 'Don't urge me to leave you…. Where you go I will go,
and where you stay I will stay. Your people will be my people, and your
God my God. Where you die, I will die, and there I will be buried'*
Ruth, talking to her mother-in-law. Ruth 1:16,17

1 SAMUEL

Overview

Samuel is the first of three 2-part books (Samuel, Kings, Chronicles) which, together with Ezra and Nehemiah, form a comprehensive history of the Israelites from their first king (Saul) to their last (Zedekiah). It introduces us to the grand old man of the Old Testament, Samuel. The book tells how the people got fed up with judges and demanded a king instead.

Despite dire predictions that he'd become a dictator, they elected Saul to be their first king. Saul was so terrified to be chosen that he hid in the locker room. That was a bad omen. A manic depressive, Saul fell apart at

---

TOP PERSONALITY – SAMUEL

Of all Old Testament leaders, Samuel never seems to put a foot wrong. He's the last judge, the first proper prophet, and the reluctant king-maker for the nation. Samuel dies the end of this book, despite Saul's attempt to spirit him back to life.

---

the emotional and spiritual seams. His favourite sport was hunting his understudy, David, who courteously refused to kill the demented old soldier. The Philistines did it instead (at Mount Gilboa).

Link to Christ

1 Samuel focuses on Israel's rejection of God as its king. God sent Samuel to give them his message, but they still wanted a human king. God sent Jesus to reclaim his sovereignty and to re-establish the 'Kingdom of God', but in a non-political and non-territorial way.

So what's the message?

The overall theme is obedience to God. We watch in admiration and horror as the 3 main characters – Samuel, Saul and David – address it.

Samuel is called to be a prophet as a child, even before he knows who God is, and his simple life-long faith becomes an example to people everywhere. Moral: you're never too young to start believing and never too old to stop serving.

David is the young shepherd boy plucked from the flock to play music to the troubled king Saul. Later, he refuses to murder the king, trusting

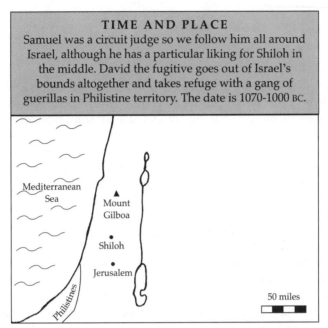
**SHILOH WAS THE FOCAL POINT OF ISRAEL'S WORSHIP –
WHERE THE TABERNACLE STOOD**

God to elevate him to the throne. Moral: be patient. Don't grab the right
thing at the wrong time in the wrong way.

Saul, in between, fails to trust God and loses his mind, his authority
and his life as a result. He makes arbitrary rules like don't eat sweets on
the battlefield, almost leading to the death of his own son (who wasn't in
assembly when the rule was announced and who helped himself to a
honeycomb). Moral: listen to advice and don't be too proud to take it.

Key verse

> *Eli said to Samuel, '...if he calls you, say, "Speak, Lord, for your
> servant is listening." '*
>
> 1 Samuel 3:10

2 SAMUEL

Overview
The story in 2 Samuel runs on from 1 Samuel (a modernising monk chopped the book in half in the fifteenth century AD) and the story is paralleled in 1 Chronicles. It tells of David's life from his accession to his old age.

David had spent a decade on the run from Saul, living as a soldier of fortune. So you might think God would have arranged an easier time for him now. He didn't. David had to put down a civil war, and then his own son Absalom (who by all accounts was a bit spoilt) attempted a coup and

---

TOP PERSONALITY – DAVID

David the Goliath-slayer and Robin Hood-prototype finally got a steady job – as king. He takes it humbly (he even grieves for Saul, when most others thanked God he'd died at last). When David fails, he accepts the fact and seeks God's forgiveness and help: a good example to us. God described David as a "man after my own heart".

David was on the run again. But David had just had his famous affair with Bathsheba, so maybe he deserved his own share of trouble and strife.

Link to Christ
To the Israelites David was the model king, who the coming Messiah would emulate. All through the Old Testament runs the messianic hope for one 'in David's line'. Jesus, as carol singers know, was born in royal David's city of birth: Bethlehem (which was actually a small village, but poets are prone to exaggerate).

So what's the message?
The book says little about God, but shows how a person can relate to God and others. David's first act was to bring the ark of the covenant into Jerusalem. It symbolised God's presence. So David was putting God at the centre of his reign, city and country. Not a bad start.

Then he went looking for Mephibosheth, the one surviving relative of his best pal Jonathan, and set him up for life. That was generous and kind,

THE UNITED KINGDOM OF DAVID

because the lad, Mephibosheth (try saying that with a mouthful of pasta) was disabled, and such people were usually dumped to beg or die.

David was a man's man (tough freedom fighter), a people's man (good king) *and* a ladies man (they just mooned over him). You don't find many people quite so all-round. He would say that's because he trusted God.

And when he made Bathsheba pregnant (and even worse, arranged her husband's death to avoid a patrimony suit), he listened to God's rebuke and said sorry. That's what God looks for, the author is saying. Humility is the first step towards spiritual maturity.

Key verse

David sang, *'The Lord is my rock, my fortress and my deliverer; my God is my rock, in whom I take refuge, my shield and the horn of my salvation.'*

2 Samuel 22:2,3

1 KINGS

Overview

1 Kings introduces Solomon, the last king of all Israel. He was only the third king, but he was still the last. After him the nation split – for ever. Solomon's son Rehoboam became greedy and tried to play power games. This drove 10 of the 12 tribes to rebel and go off with a disenchanted former civil servant. They became known as Israel, and were the northerners.

That left just the 2 southern tribes (Judah and Simeon) to follow Rehoboam (who had no power left to play with) and they became known as Judah.

TOP PERSONALITY – ELIJAH

Elijah is the Bible's first real miracle worker (apart from a few minor incidents like Moses parting the Red Sea). Elijah is one of the real characters of the Bible. His greatest miracle was calling down God's fire on a sacrifice on Mount Carmel, to show God was alive and kindling, whereas the idols were dead and inert. Elijah had his failings too, his most magnificent failure was running away in a fit of self-pitying depression straight after his amazing triumph at Mount Carmel, instead of posing for the cameras. Spiritual 'highs' are often followed by spiritual lows – but God spoke to him in a new, softer way, which humbled the great man. We must listen out for the still small voice of God.

After Solomon's death, the story in 1 Kings focuses mostly on Israel and the prophet Elijah.

Link to Christ

Elijah met Christ on the Mount of Transfiguration. The Bible regards Elijah as the epitome of the prophets and in later Jewish thought Elijah was expected to reappear before the Messiah came. Jesus described John the Baptist as 'Elijah': someone with the same message (not to mention the same life-style – they both wore camel coats and lived off unmentionable things in the desert).

So what does it all mean?

The book of 1 Kings hammers home the moral tales – like Aussie batsmen

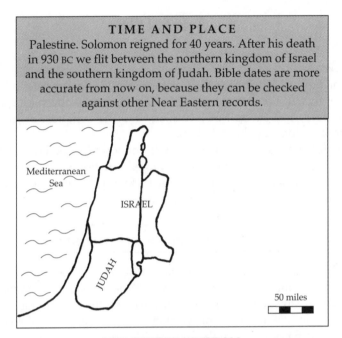

TIME AND PLACE

Palestine. Solomon reigned for 40 years. After his death in 930 BC we flit between the northern kingdom of Israel and the southern kingdom of Judah. Bible dates are more accurate from now on, because they can be checked against other Near Eastern records.

Mediterranean Sea

ISRAEL

JUDAH

50 miles

THE DIVIDED KINGDOM

driving England's bowlers to the boundary. It starts with Solomon doing the right thing by asking God for wisdom instead of wealth. (He got both, as it happened.) We admire him. And we're meant to emulate him.

King Ahab is the beast to King Solomon's beauty. Ahab married a bitch called Jezebel who everyone hated; she ruled the roost. She brought her foreign gods and priests with her, and then tried to do away with Israel's God. Elijah stood up to her, and God protected him. (and we're meant to emulate Elijah, too.)

So after a catalogue of religious disobedience, moral depravity and plain old fashioned greed, Ahab bled painfully to death and the story moves on. The author wants us to see that sin doesn't pay. It only encourages other people to sin us back; doing to others as we are done by is one of humankind's less attractive habits.

Key verse

'How long will you waver between two opinions? If the Lord is God, follow him; but if Baal is God, follow him.'
Elijah speaking to all Israel on Mount Carmel 1 Kings 18:21

2 KINGS

Overview

This book boils down 250 years of history into 25 short chapters. It tells of the fall of Samaria and the conquest of Israel (the northern kingdom) by the Assyrians, and the fall of Jerusalem and the conquest of Judah (the southern kingdom) by the Babylonians.

It's a bit like watching a 'sit com' with the sound turned down; you see rapid changes of scene and camera angle, but you've got to be really sharp to follow the story. The account flicks rapidly between Israel and Judah, and treats most of the kings as extras.

TOP PERSONALITY – KING JOSIAH

Josiah reigned over Judah for 30 years (640-609 BC) was only 8 when he became king. At the ripe old age of 26 he launched a massive re-form of Judah's religious life which staved off the impending doom. The reform took off when his workmen rediscovered the Bible (or a bit of it) gathering dust in the Temple. It's a powerful book.

Israel had 19 kings, all of them bad. Judah had 20 kings, only 8 of them good. They included *Hezekiah* (a panic-stricken nice guy who ran around crying, 'Don't panic!') and *Josiah* who sorted out the chaos of his predecessors two centuries too late. *Jehu* (in Israel) was dramatically bad (the prototype road-rager whose chariot driving was infamous and whose murder record rivalled Hitler's).

Link to Christ

Josiah's men found Deuteronomy which balances law (what you must do) and grace (God's compassionate love even for those who don't keep the law, emphasising the need to be compassionate to one another). So the events of 2 Kings prepare people for Christ's teaching almost 600 years later.

So what's the message?

The author was writing for the people of Judea, who had been exiled to Babylon from about 600 BC onwards (there were several deportations). He is telling them two things. First, *how* both Israel and Judah fell from grace, and secondly, *why* God seemed to have abandoned them.

TIME LINE

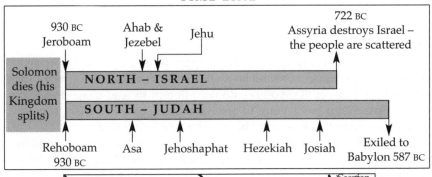

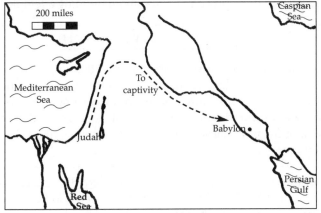

JUDAH EXILED TO BABYLON

We can see why God was so displeased when we see how they displeased him. It was like a married peson openly sleeping around. They had agreed to worship God, and yet they did the rounds of all the superstitions and cults as well.

Both Israel and Judah fell because they didn't live in the way God had told them. So they reaped the consequences. You can't expect to gorge junk food and stay slim; you can't expect to ignore God and stay spiritually fit; in fact, you get everything out of perspective.

Key verse

> 'Go and enquire of the Lord for me and for the people...about what is written in this book that has been found. Great is the Lord's anger that burns against us because our fathers have not obeyed the words of this book.'
>
> King Josiah in 2 Kings 22:13

1 CHRONICLES

Overview

I Chronicles is mostly about David, apart from all the lists of names (which, in passing, do remind us that history is made up of more than kings). So whatever else you do, do not attempt to read chapters 1-9 and 23-27. Censorship has a place in a civilised society, and I wish to protect you from a terrible fate – you'll be bored out of your mind.

This book is a repeat performance of 2 Samuel (with some additions such as a psalm and some lists). We're back in the time of king David, taking over from Saul and dreaming big dreams about building a temple for God.

TOP PERSONALITY – DAVID

David is the only personality (apart from 2,000 unpronounceable names) and so gets his second star on the pavement of honour. Chronicles stresses his faith (and even quotes one of his psalms) and his God-centredness. David's chief concern is the church. Everything fits in to his scheme, and yet nothing suffers. There's a moral there.

The chronicler isn't simply a copier, however. His concern is to write the history of the temple and to show to what extent God's people obeyed God. So David is flavour of the month.

Link to Christ

The temple which David plans is the first of 3 which will grace Jerusalem in the next 1,000 years. Jesus looked at the third, and said, 'Destroy this temple and I'll raise it up in three days.' He was referring to the 'temple' of his body, and reminding everyone that there's one structure more important to God than a place of worship.

So what's the message?

For most of us, church is for marking rites of passage we could do without: baptisms of children to please grandparents, funerals we curse God for making necessary, and weddings which half the population doesn't see the need for.

For David and the Chronicler, 'church' was not just a club for the faithful or the religious wing of the social services. The temple was a focal point

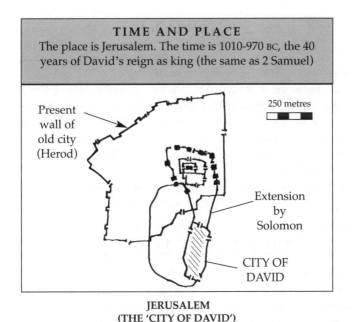

Present
wall of
old city
(Herod)

250 metres

Extension
by
Solomon

CITY OF
DAVID

JERUSALEM
(THE 'CITY OF DAVID')

for the nation's spiritual life. It was the equivalent of Westminster Abbey
and the Palace of Westminster, because for the Israelites there was no
sacred-secular divide.

They saw the whole world as God's; he was its ultimate ruler. He
deserved the best of worship (defined as godly living and not just
religious rites) before they sorted out their quarrels with the Philistines. It
was a different world-view. We'll see it again when we get to Jesus.

Key verse

*Give thanks to the Lord, call on his name; make known among the
nations what he has done. Sing to him, sing praise to him; tell of all his
wonderful acts.*

David, in 1 Chronicles 16:8,9

2 CHRONICLES

Overview

The break between 1 and 2 Chronicles occurred when the Jews were translating their Hebrew Bible into Greek in the second century BC, possibly because 2 scrolls were easier to handle than one long one.

2 Chronicles parallels the story in 1 and 2 Kings from the life of Solomon to the capture of Jerusalem by the Babylonians and the destruction of the temple.

After the division of the kingdom, this book focuses entirely on Judah, the southern kingdom, with its main concern being the temple and

---

TOP PERSONALITY – SOLOMON

What would you ask if your fairy godmother granted you one wish? God made Solomon that offer, and Solomon asked for wisdom instead of wealth. Whether you judge him brave or stupid depends on your viewpoint, but he had the last laugh: he got both.

---

religious life. Kings are judged as good or bad entirely on whether they follow the Lord or other gods.

This book is pretty selective. The Greek translators called Chronicles 'Things missing' (missing from the other books). And, praise God, there's no more lists of names.

Link to Christ

The villain of this book is king Manasseh. He turned the temple into a New Age fair, and burnt his own sons at the stake of some pagan God. Then he got kicked in his manly pride and carted off to Babylon as a prisoner of war. While there he said sorry to God. He was let out on remand and cleaned up his act. Remember the penitent thief on the cross next to Jesus? You're never too bad and it's never too late to turn back to God.

So what's the message?

The Chronicler loves Solomon, despite the fact that Solomon had 700 wives and 300 concubines (which the Chronicler generously overlooks). The great king can do no wrong in his eyes, and all succeeding kings are measured against Solomon's standard.

THE 3 TEMPLES AT JERUSALEM

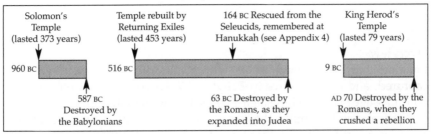

| Solomon's Temple (lasted 373 years) | Temple rebuilt by Returning Exiles (lasted 453 years) | 164 BC Rescued from the Seleucids, remembered at Hanukkah (see Appendix 4) | King Herod's Temple (lasted 79 years) |

960 BC   516 BC   9 BC

587 BC Destroyed by the Babylonians   63 BC Destroyed by the Romans, as they expanded into Judea   AD 70 Destroyed by the Romans, when they crushed a rebellion

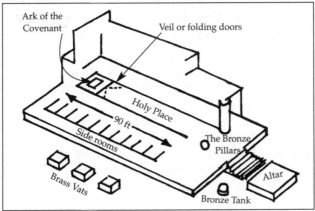

SOLOMON'S TEMPLE

Solomon's redeeming virtues were that, like David his father, he put God first. And he was kindly and good to people, too. (The fact that he devised an economic system which actually worked in everyone's favour is seen as a a minor point.) He appreciated beauty, patronised the arts, and spent hours in his garden studying nature.

No wonder the Queen of Sheba fancied him. (Rumours that he sired her son are not supported in the Bible.) His priorities were God, people's welfare, and a holistic lifestyle. Got that?

(PS Don't try to emulate his marital exploits; even if they didn't wear him out they *did* contribute to the decline and fall of the next generation.)

Key verse

'Give me wisdom and knowledge, that I may lead this people, for who is able to govern this great people of yours?'
Solomon, in 2 Chronicles 1:10

EZRA

Overview

Imagine that you belong to an ethnic minority family, and you are captured, and forced to live in Babylon. When your captors offer to pay your passage home (to Jerusalem) you set off with high hopes.

Your aim is to rebuild the temple, the symbol of your national and religious identity. But it's hard work. The local people regard you as foreigners, not relations. They don't share your ideals. They oppose you. And just try finding that patch of land which granddad farmed seventy

---

TOP PERSONALITY – EZRA

Ezra the priest. He appears halfway through the book named after him, 60 years after the temple was rebuilt. He refused an armed escort for the long journey, an act of faith somewhat over-shadowed by his legally correct but pastorally painful insistence on the mass divorce of Jews from women of other races.

---

years ago. Ezra is the true story of how the Jews overcame obstacles to build the second temple.

Link to Christ

Ezra, among others, laid the foundations for the religious system of synagogues and scribes (teachers of the law) found in the New Testament. The book itself is an illustration of Jesus' teaching that God can bring new life and hope to people who are spiritually weary and heavy laden.

So what's the message?

Ezra shows that God keeps his promises. The prophet Jeremiah (and others) had predicted an exile of Jews in Babylon lasting 70 years. Ezra shows that God had it written in his planner and didn't forget the date: the first return in 537 BC was virtually 70 years from the first deportation (there were others later) in 605 BC.

That also shows that God takes a longer term view of life than today's newspapers. But since we live in a society that generally prefers instant coffee to the real thing (which only takes five minutes to brew) this could

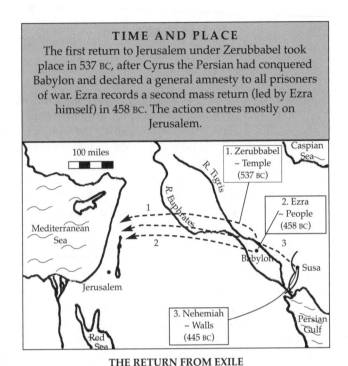

TIME AND PLACE

The first return to Jerusalem under Zerubbabel took place in 537 BC, after Cyrus the Persian had conquered Babylon and declared a general amnesty to all prisoners of war. Ezra records a second mass return (led by Ezra himself) in 458 BC. The action centres mostly on Jerusalem.

100 miles

1. Zerubbabel
~ Temple
(537 BC)

Caspian Sea

R. Tigris

R. Euphrates

2. Ezra
~ People
(458 BC)

Mediterranean Sea

Babylon

Susa

Jerusalem

3. Nehemiah
~ Walls
(445 BC)

Persian Gulf

Red Sea

THE RETURN FROM EXILE

be a hard lesson to swallow. We might have to wait years to see answers to our prayers. We might also discover that God isn't choosy about who he uses to bring the answers. The release from captivity – and the authorisation to build the temple – came through a pagan king, not a swashbuckling messiah.

Key verse

With praise and thanksgiving they sang to the Lord: 'He is good; his love to Israel endures for ever.'

Ezra 3:11

NEHEMIAH

Overview

Nehemiah was a winetaster. Winetasting is an ancient art, but in Nehemiah's time people didn't do it for a column in a newspaper, but to check that the chalice wasn't poisoned – before the king took a swig. Nehemiah lived dangerously. So he was just the guy to return from Persia to Jerusalem to rebuild the city walls.

Because re-building the walls was dangerous too. Local bigwigs didn't want to see the restoration of the walls, and issued death threats against the upstart builder. But Nehemiah did it, and he enlisted Ezra's help to

---

TOP PERSONALITY – NEHEMIAH

The book is based on Nehemiah's personal diary. Apart from being secretive, confident, bossy and pragmatic – all essential characteristics of a leader – Nehemiah was also a man of intense faith. For him, God was always around and always involved.

---

rededicate the city to God. And with that, the Old Testament narrative ends. Christ will be born nearby, 450 years later.

Link to Christ

Nehemiah is like the French Carmelite monk Brother Lawrence who wrote a book that's still in print called *The Practice of the Presence of God*. Lawrence's spiritual habit was to pray to God anywhere because God was, well, everywhere. He got the idea from Jesus, but Nehemiah had it first.

So what's the message?

The rebuilding of the walls of Jerusalem was an important event in Jewish history. But it's Nehemiah's method rather than his achievement that contains the message. He invented what Christians sometimes call 'arrow prayers'; whenever he got in a tight spot he shot one up. God was, and is, a good management consultant.

And Nehemiah didn't close his eyes or fold his hands, either (unlike the Brazilian goalkeeper who let in a goal after three seconds because he was still saying his prayers). He reckoned prayer and action were

WALLS OF JERUSALEM REBUILT BY NEHEMIAH

compatible and necessary. So he took physical as well as spiritual precautions to protect his workforce. He worked with a trowel in one hand and a sword in the other, to keep his enemies at bay. When the job was done he was installed as governor, and let Ezra lead the celebration service. He was what Bible writers call 'wise'. A good act to follow.

Key verse

We prayed to our God and posted a guard day and night to meet this threat. ... So the wall was completed in 52 days. When all our enemies heard about this, all the surrounding nations were afraid and lost their confidence, because they realised that this work had been done with the help of our God.

Nehemiah 4:9, and 6:15, 16

ESTHER

Overview
The story of Esther would make a great Hollywood film. It is a sanctified version of Cinderella with sex-appeal, attempted murder and political intrigue. Esther was a beautiful orphaned Jewish girl (brought up by her older cousin Mordecai) shipped off into the royal harem, given extensive beauty treatments (while hiding her nationality) and ended up as the queen. Meanwhile Mordecai uncovers a fiendish plot hatched by a royal official called Haman to destroy the Jewish people. Esther found the courage to stop the evil plan.

TOP PERSONALITY – ESTHER

Queen Esther kept silent about her true identity and ended up well-placed to act on behalf of her people, when the chips were down. She risked her place in the royal bed, and her life, in order to save the Jewish people from destruction. (Even a queen could be sentenced to death for speaking to the king without permission – silly, but those were the rules).

Esther decided to throw a party to catch the evil Haman. After considerable legal wrangling Haman literally gets hoist on his own petard (a gallows intended for Mordecai) and all (except Haman) live happily ever after.

Link to Christ
The story of Esther is another example of 'salvation' or God's rescue, which Jesus also offers. The Jews celebrate their rescue from Haman each year in the festival of Purim, when everyone boos Haman and cheers Mordecai. It's great fun. Unfortunately this festival is not mentioned in the New Testament, but Jesus probably enjoyed it in his own day.

So what's the message?
The book of Esther is unique in the Bible: it doesn't mention God. But he's there, hovering like a shadow over the events and giving a superb example of what the theologians call 'providence'. The right people are in the right place at the right time – and, mercifully, they do the right thing.

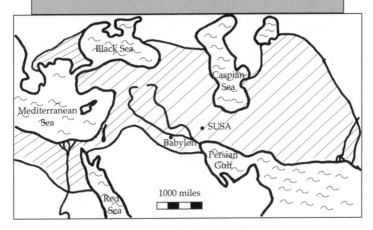

THE PERSIAN EMPIRE

Through the events, God is seen to be guiding and protecting the fortunes of his people.

As in life, God does seem a bit distant and his activity is only seen clearly in retrospect. It turns into a story about faith; God can be trusted not to let some tyrant completely wipe out his people. It's the story of the Jews, and of the Christian church, in microcosm; the gates of hell, said Jesus, can't prevail against God's work. They still try, but that's their problem.

Key verse

Mordecai [was]... held in high esteem by his many fellow Jews, because he worked for the good of his people and spoke up for the welfare of all the Jews.

Esther 10:3

JOB

Overview

The book of Job is the Bible's answer to the age-old question 'Why do bad things happen to good people?' Before you read it though, note 2 things. First, the man's name is pronounced Jobe (like Joe with a cold, not 'job' as in work). Secondly, most of the book is rubbish. That's not my verdict, but Job's – and God's.

This book is full of the sort of vacuous waffle people gush out when they don't understand. Here's poor Job, a godly man who loses everything in what insurers would call an act of God (actually, it was an act of Satan)

TOP PERSONALITY – JOB

Seeing that the 4 debaters in this book get a thick ear from God, that only leaves Job to fill the slot for 'top personality'. Job had a lot of bottle, because he stuck to his guns. But he also suffered from spiritual short sight like the rest of us. He forgot just how great God is. He was a good man, though. And he was given everything back in the end.

---

and is smitten with some loathsome skin complaint. All he wants is a hug and bit of sympathy. You can understand them avoiding the hug, but instead of sympathy he gets blame. Because if you suffer, you're a sinner, they said (still a commonly held belief, deep down). Job objects, and the debate begins.

Link to Christ

If ever there was a truly innocent sufferer, it was Jesus Christ. 'Led like a lamb to the slaughter,' the Bible says (in a hymn-writer's paraphrase). He never complained, and saw it as his mission because through his innocent suffering, he atoned for the world's evil.

So what's the message?

Quite simply, there's no fixed penalty for sin in the world. Which unfortunately means that innocent people suffer sometimes and bad people don't suffer enough. If you get sick, lose your partner, go bankrupt

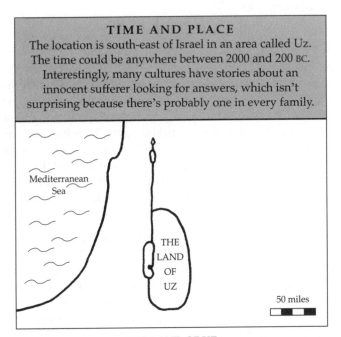

TIME AND PLACE
The location is south-east of Israel in an area called Uz.
The time could be anywhere between 2000 and 200 BC.
Interestingly, many cultures have stories about an
innocent sufferer looking for answers, which isn't
surprising because there's probably one in every family.

Mediterranean
Sea

THE
LAND
OF
UZ

50 miles

THE LAND OF UZ

through someone else's bloody-mindedness, or suffer in any way, it's just bad luck. God hasn't got a downer on you.

Job suggests that the answer to 'the problem of suffering' is beyond human comprehension *but not beyond God's*. The rest of the Bible shows that the God (whose own son suffered horribly) has a special place in his heart for all who suffer. CS Lewis said suffering was 'God's megaphone to rouse a deaf world'. It reminds us that there's something very wrong with the world. It concentrates the mind on the essentials. Like just how fragile (and beautiful) life is, and how we ought to make space for God. And not shout platitudes in sufferers' ears.

Key verse

'Shall we accept good from God, and not trouble?' In all this, Job did not sin in what he said.

Job 2:10

PSALMS

Overview

The book of psalms is the Hebrew prayer book. It is an anthology of religious poetry written by many people and covers most aspects of human life. There's no order to it, so you may go from agony to ecstasy in a few lines. Some of it is prayer or praise, some is outpouring of feeling, and some is poetic recounting of events. 75 of the 150 psalms were written by king David, who knew all about the highs and lows of life.

But be warned: it doesn't rhyme. Hebrew poetry works by comparing, contrasting or developing *ideas* in what is known as 'parallelism'. For

---

TOP PERSONALITY – GOD

We had to give God the top spot some time. While many psalms recount human exploits, their chief theme is the goodness and faithfulness of God even (perhaps especially) in the dark days of suffering. 'His love endures for ever' is a refrain to Psalm 118 but is the chief theme of the book.

---

example, 'The Lord is a refuge for the oppressed, a stronghold in times of trouble' (9:9) puts one idea in two ways. But you'll get more out of the book if you think about what it means, not how it's constructed.

Link to Christ

Some of the psalms are 'prophetic' and express sentiments that were later applied to Christ. One quoted several times in the New Testament is Psalm 110 ('The Lord (God) says to my Lord, sit at my right hand') in reference to Christ's divinity and ascension.

So what's the message?

The figurative language ('the mountains skipped like rams,' 114:4) is meant to lift us above the material world and to remind us that there are things we can't understand and there are truths which are bigger than our prosaic definitions. Beauty is not just chemistry, love is not just feelings, and God is not made in the image of humankind and does not act according to human wisdom.

Like all good poetry, the psalms put into words our otherwise inex-

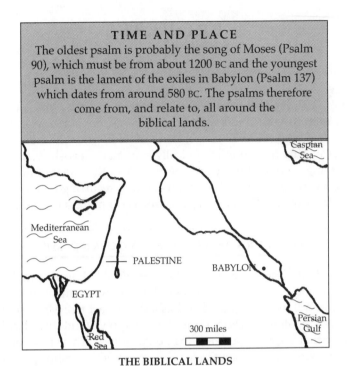

Caspian Sea

Mediterranean Sea

PALESTINE

BABYLON •

EGYPT

Persian Gulf

300 miles

Red Sea

THE BIBLICAL LANDS

pressible thoughts and feelings. Most of them are prayer and worship, but don't be surprised at occasional outbursts of rage; it's not all stained glass piety. God can absorb and understand our anger. There's a handful of really nasty ones too ('May his days be few' 109:8 and 'happy is he who repays you for what you have done to us – he who seizes your infants and dashes them against the rocks' 137:9) which speak of the longing for justice. They stem from a belief that God is just, even though life is a bitch.

Key verse

The Lord is the great God, the great King above all gods. In his hand are the depths of the earth, and the mountain peaks belong to him.
Psalm 95:3,4

PROVERBS

Overview
The book of Proverbs opens with words that will take you back a few years: 'Listen to your dad's advice...'. By now, of course, you probably wish you had, and are tearing your hair out while your children disregard *your* advice. This collection of typically pragmatic Jewish wisdom starts with warnings about adultery but covers many other areas of life too.

The proverbs are jumbled but there are four recurring themes: wisdom is better than wealth (it lasts longer); words do more damage than wars

---

TOP PERSONALITIES – YOU AND ME

Some double acts are especially memorable (Punch and Judy, Morecambe and Wise, Little and Large). Sometimes you can't separate a double act. Proverbs has a double act too: Mr Wiseman and Mr Foolhead. They stand for everyone (and the divided nature that we all experience inside ourselves). Their reactions to real-life scenarios are contrasted. There are no prizes for guessing which one we're supposed to emulate.

(so don't prattle); be nice to your neighbour (someone's got to); work hard (there are no free lunches). Nothing changes.

Link to Christ
The book of Proverbs personifies wisdom, (especially in chapter 8). It makes wisdom seem almost godlike. That's not so surprising when you recall that Jesus described himself as 'the truth' and Paul called him 'the wisdom of God'. To err is human; wisdom is divine.

So what's the message?
Basically, prudence prospers and folly fails. We all know there are exceptions (the compilers know it too and tell us not to fret when the wicked get away with it), but the message is best summed up by the modern Chief Rabbi Jonathan Sacks. He wrote that moral wisdom is to be cherished 'because life is short, and the bill for our mistakes is long.'

Proverbs is an antidote to the human habit of pushing barriers until

TIME AND PLACE

King Solomon (he who wisely advocated cutting a child in two to settle a dispute between two mothers who both claimed it, knowing the real mother would cry 'no') is credited with some of this book, and he lived about 950 BC. King Hezekiah edited some of it. Other named compilers are unknown. But they were all Israelites.

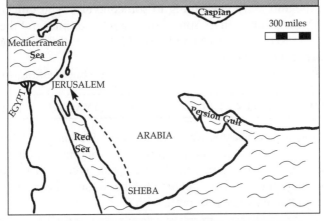

THE QUEEN OF SHEBA VISITED SOLOMON AND WAS AMAZED AT HIS WEALTH AND WISDOM

they break, of going too far, of trying to get away with what we can. There's no point in being rich if you don't use riches wisely. You'll end up unhappy and leave a trail of trouble behind you. Slagging people off may make you feel good but it only adds to the sum of human misery and will rebound on you. The world will only be a nicer place if you start being nice. Simple common sense, really.

Key verse

Pride goes before destruction, a haughty spirit before a fall.
Proverbs 16:18

ECCLESIASTES

Overview

Now here's a surprise: a Bible book written by someone who has departed from the path of faith, wandered down the by-ways of agnosticism and arrived in the cul-de-sac of aimlessness. You work hard for years, die and leave everything to someone else who quickly forgets you. What's the point in that? You go out for a good time, and then all you want (after a rest) is – another good time. Nothing satisfies us for long, so what's the point of anything?

This is a book to concentrate the mind on The Meaning of Life. Its

---

TOP PERSONALITY – THE ANONYMOUS KING

The King in Ecclesiastes was a lucky man. He had the leisure to learn about life, rather than focus on survival. He had the money to build palaces and parks (and a harem as well). On top of sex and money, he also had power. But he wasn't the first or last person in history to be miserable with it.

---

punchline is that maybe serving God isn't such a bad idea after all.

Link to Christ

Jesus said seek God's kingdom first, and you'll get by and be satisfied. That's the punch-line here, too. Jesus might have read Ecclesiastes shortly before he preached the Sermon on the Mount. Wordsworth made the same point in his poem 'The world is too much with us' when he wrote 'getting and spending we lay waste our powers'.

So what's the message?

The message is best summed up in the famous poem of chapter 3 which starts, 'There is a time for everything.' Ecclesiastes is about balance. Of course you've got to work, it says – but don't become a workaholic. Leisure is good, but it's not the sole purpose of life; there's a time to weep as well as a time to laugh (because you care about the world's ills, don't you?).

With the stress on balance comes a call to contentment. 'He who has money never has money enough' (5:10) ought to be written over the desks

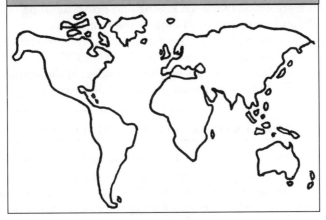

THE WORLD
['everything is meaningless' (1:2, 12:8)]

of Wall Street traders not as an incentive but as a warning. You can have too much of a good thing. And then it starts to possess you; it becomes your master not your servant. That's a fate worse than death. So he ends: 'remember your creator in the days of your youth' – before it's too late (12:1).

Key verse

I hated all the things I had toiled for under the sun, because I must leave them to the one who comes after me. And who knows whether he will be a wise man or a fool?

Ecclesiastes 2:18,19

SONG OF SONGS

Overview

The Song of Songs is a dialogue between two lovers. This is the book that a former generation giggled over in scripture lessons. It's not exactly steamy, but there's a bit of French kissing and breast fondling between the covers, and there are some veiled hints at the Full Monty.

Interpreters have had a field day with this. It has been presented as an allegory (of the relationship between Christ and the church) or as a religious drama. But frankly, it's just a celebration of the sexuality that is part of creation – with the emphasis on beauty and wonder.

TOP PERSONALITIES – THE LOVERS

The man (the 'lover') is tender and devoted. The woman (the 'beloved') is longing for her man. She goes searching for him. She describes him in endearing terms ('I belong to my lover, and his desire is for me'). She is in love with him for himself, not for what she can get from him. Restores your faith in human nature.

Most modern versions (such as the NIV) tell you who is speaking in each section – the lover or the beloved. There is also a group of friends watching and chanting a chorus (which is probably a literary device, but it makes you think!).

Link to Christ

The allegory idea is not so daft as it sounds, because Paul uses sexual union as a picture of the intimate relationship between Christ and his church: there is a deep bond, not just a nodding acquaintance. Besides, it's worth recalling that Christ was never disparaging about sexuality.

So what's the message?

You need to put this book in the context of the rest of the Bible (which is an important principle of biblical interpretation anyway). Sex was invented by God, according to Genesis (and that's never denied anywhere else), therefore like the rest of the original creation it is a Good Thing. However, it's never been easy to handle and people through the ages have

Present wall of old city (Herod)

250 metres

Royal Palace Gardens

JERUSALEM IN SOLOMON'S TIME

handled it pretty badly. So in places the Bible gives some stern warnings about adultery, fornication and the rest. They are a misuse of a gift which symbolises (and creates) a deep emotional, spiritual and physical bond.

So the Song celebrates sexuality at its best. Here is the innocent beauty of physical love demonstrated in the context of love for a whole person by a whole person. It is exclusive, endearing and enduring. It makes you wonder why we settle for less.

Key verse

He has taken me to the banquet hall, and his banner over me is love.
Song of Songs 2:4

53

ISAIAH

Overview

Isaiah is the prince of the prophets. Old Testament prophecy is daunting if you're new to it, so this is a good place to start. Begin by reading chapters 40-55 first. They are just majestic poetry and magnificent theology. (Handel used bits of it for *The Messiah*.) While relating to a historical situation, they are utterly timeless and reveal God's greatness.

Chapters 1-39 relate to a period of religious and social decline in Judah (the southern of the two Israelite kingdoms). They describe God's horror at sin, and promised judgement of it. And they show Isaiah as a court adviser bolstering King Hezekiah's faltering faith in God.

TOP PERSONALITY – ISAIAH

Isaiah is a towering figure of faith. He may have belonged to a leading family, and certainly had access to the corridors of power. His poetry is brilliant and he introduced people of his time to a view of God which lifted him above the tribal level to that of Lord of the universe. It all began with a spine-tingling vision of God that was at once both awesome and encouraging.

Link to Christ

Chapter 53 describes the 'suffering servant'. While capable of other applications, the chapter clearly finds its greatest fulfilment in the life, death and resurrection of Jesus. Other passages point forward to Christ too, such as 7.14 ('The virgin will be with child...and will call him Immanuel') and 9.6 ('unto us a child is born ... and he will be called wonderful counsellor') which are often read at Christmas carol services.

So what's the message?

God is bigger than we think. Some of the poems portray God as the supreme creator, sustainer and saviour of all. This is also implied in Isaiah's dealings with Hezekiah, quaking in his shoes as the Assyrians battered on the door of Jerusalem. 'Don't worry, my son,' Isaiah told him. 'Trust God and don't do anything stupid like making a military alliance with the Egyptians.' The message is that God is big enough to look after our interests without us having to take panic measures.

TIME AND PLACE

Chapters 1-39 relate to 750-700 BC. Israel (the northern ten tribes) was destroyed in 722 BC by the Assyrians who also threatened but did not destroy Judah (the southern two tribes). Chapters 40-66 relate to Judah's later exile in Babylon (about 600-500 BC) and were either written by someone else or are an example of 'fore-telling'.

THE ASSYRIAN EMPIRE AND THE THREAT FROM THE ASSYRIANS

There is a superb vision of heaven, too, stressing God's holiness. Balanced against that is a picture of a God who cares. Despite outspoken condemnation of social sins like oppression and corruption, Isaiah shows God yearning for his people like a jilted lover. God is high and mighty, but he loves to spend time with ordinary people who know their spiritual poverty and don't try and do his job.

Key verse

This is what the Lord says... 'I live in a high and holy place, but also with those who are contrite and lowly in spirit, to revive the spirit of the lowly and to revive the heart of the contrite.'

Isaiah 57:15

JEREMIAH

Overview

Jeremiah is remembered as the 'weeping prophet' and he has lent his name to a range of moaning minnies who get dubbed 'Jeremiahs'. For Winnie the Pooh fans, Jeremiah is Eeyore, full of doom and gloom. Optimists will try to avoid this book.

In fact, Jeremiah told the truth and was hated for it. He could see that Judah was inviting God's judgement by its corporate behaviour, which was hardly what people wanted to know. This, the longest book in the Bible, is a hotchpotch of unrelated messages in no particular order, which

---

TOP PERSONALITY – JEREMIAH

Jeremiah was in a job he hated. He felt compelled to speak God's hard words even though he was a sensitive soul who shrank from conflict and was prone to depression. He wears his heart on his sleeve, and provides a magnificent example of someone who put duty before desire.

---

makes it harder to understand. But you get glimpses of God's love shining above, and even through, the gloomy clouds.

Link to Christ

Jesus also had a pessimistic streak and talked more about hell than heaven – a fact often overlooked by those who prefer the image of a gentle shepherd in a field of flowers. Like Jeremiah, Jesus called on people to 'repent', that is to turn away from self-centred living, to put God first.

So what's the message?

Jeremiah only ever had two things to say, although he found an almost infinite number of ways to say them. The first was that God cannot tolerate taking second place in anyone's life; that, in effect, makes something or someone else god in his place. Seeing that people were created to live in harmony with him, chaos can only ensue as a result of failing to.

The second was that turning back to God might avert the catastrophe (he advocated submission to the Babylonians which seemed suicidal to

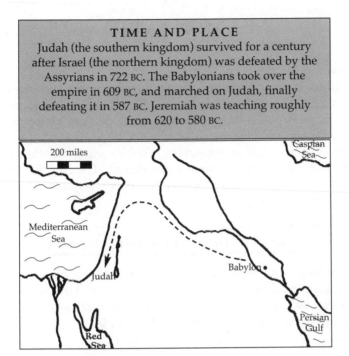

200 miles

Caspian Sea

Mediterranean Sea

Judah

Babylon •

Persian Gulf

Red Sea

THE BABYLONIANS ATTACK JUDAH

less faithful people). He showed that God allows people to reap the results of their folly only reluctantly, and that he gives ample opportunity to pull back from the brink. And when we fail to and the judgement bites, there is still hope of a new start with him if we ask humbly for it.

Key verse

> 'For I know the plans I have for you,' declares the Lord, 'plans to prosper you and not to harm you, plans to give you hope and a future. Then you will call upon me and come and pray to me, and I will listen to you.'
>
> Jeremiah 29:11,12

LAMENTATIONS

Overview

Lamentations is about emotions – grief, remorse, anger and frustration. If men don't cry, they may go and break something, or kill someone. It's better to express powerful emotions in a manner less violent and more cathartic. That is what the writer of Lamentations is doing. The cause of his distress is the fall of Jerusalem. The invading Babylonians have brought lawlessness, theft, famine and suffering. It seems like the end of the world. This short book is divided into 5 poems – and is something of a Hebrew literary masterpiece.

TOP PERSONALITY – THE AUTHOR

The author is anonymous. Tradition points to Jeremiah who was uniquely placed to write this and whose own book is full of angst. Whoever he was, he deserves a medal for honesty and bravery as he bares his soul and identifies with his people.

Link to Christ

Jesus himself mourned over Jerusalem, seeing ahead to the days (some 40 years later) when it would once again be destroyed and its temple demolished (which happened in AD 70 at the hands of the Romans). Jesus also wept over it, longing for its people to respond to God's call to trust in him once more.

So what's the message?

That it's OK to cry, especially if you pray at the same time. If God can't understand and empathise, no-one can. He's heard worse things than your cries of pain. But notice that the author isn't just crying for himself. Certainly he has suffered personally, but he is also crying for his city and his nation.

He identifies with the sufferings of his people. He is personally innocent, yet mourns for those who have contributed to this disaster by their faithless lifestyles. This is empathy par excellence, and a strong antidote to today's shoulder-shrugging individualism ('they probably deserved it – it's not my business to get involved'). Sorrow is expressed so

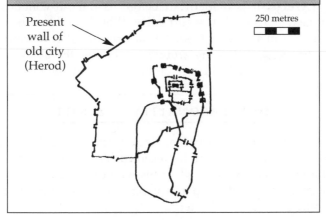

Present
wall of
old city
(Herod)

250 metres

JERUSALEM IN 600 BC

powerfully and poetically here, we can use it to put our own sorrow into words. This is a book to use, not just to read.

Key verse

Because of the Lord's great love we are not consumed, for his compassions never fail. They are new every morning; great is your faithfulness.

Lamentations 3:22,23

59

EZEKIEL

Overview

This book is proof that the Bible combines the sublime and the ridiculous (just like life). The story of Ezekiel would not be out of place on the Edinburgh Fringe. It is modern art before its time. It contains abstract images of God portrayed in weird ways. Wheels within wheels (full of eyes) symbolise an all-seeing God. A Dali-like surreal graveyard in which dry dusty bones start dancing around symbolises the ability of God to bring us new life. Ezekiel's bizarre performance lying on his side for over

---

TOP PERSONALITY – EZEKIEL

Ezekiel was a priest in Babylon. He was among the first exiles to be taken to Babylon where he received his call to prophesy. He was happily married, and when his wife died God ordered him not to mourn as another 'performance' to convey a message. He was courageous and dedicated.

---

a year in front of a model village was a warning to prepare the people for a long drawn-out siege of Jerusalem. Ezekiel would make some modern artists look almost normal. But if you have the eye of an artist, you'll find the book contains some profound ideas.

Link to Christ

Ezekiel's opening vision has some similarities with that of the apostle John in the book of Revelation. John saw Christ on the heavenly throne; Ezekiel sees 'the likeness of the glory of the Lord', which is much the same thing.

So what's the message?

Ezekiel shows that God will go to any lengths to get his message across. It is too important to be wrapped up in literary niceties and scientific experiments. It's so urgent that it must risk mis-interpretation in order to attract attention and be heard by all groups of society. It's an early example of the strategy used by St Paul, to 'become all things to all people'. God isn't fussy, which is just as well for us.

Ezekiel also introduces us to the mysteries of the universe. God can be

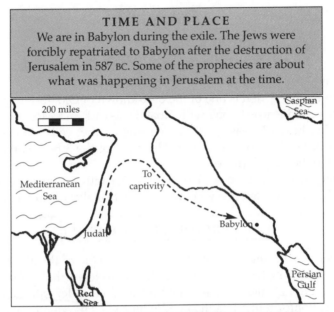

EZEKIEL WAS TAKEN TO CAPTIVITY IN BABYLON

perceived through symbol and image. We cannot reduce him to a neat
formula on the blackboard nor contain him in a can for mass con-
sumption. He is a holy God to be approached with awe, but one who also
has compassion on his people. Ezekiel stresses that each individual is
called to respond to God personally.

Key verse

*This is what the Sovereign Lord says: I myself will search for my sheep
and look after them...I will search for the lost and bring back the strays.
I will bind up the injured and strengthen the weak, but the sleek I will
destroy. I will shepherd the flock with justice.*
Ezekiel 34:11,16

DANIEL

Overview

Daniel in the lions' den is one of the best-known of Old Testament stories that every child learns (along with Noah in the ark and Moses in the bulrushes). Belshazzar's feast (with the writing on the wall) originates from the book of Daniel too, and as does the story of the 3 holy children who stay cool in the fiery furnace.

Daniel is a 2-part book. Part one is narrative (with the unusual stories that no-one is sure whether or not to believe) and part two is

---

TOP PERSONALITY – DANIEL

Daniel was daring. The pioneering *Eagle* comic of the 1950s was initiated by a Christian, so it may be no accident that it featured 'Dan Dare'. Daniel remained faithful to God under intense pressure to conform to a less than godly lifestyle. His enemies were as evil as the Mekon, but his secret weapon of regular doses of prayer toppled them from their pedestals.

'apocalyptic', which is a posh word for way-out prophecy that describes the 'end times' in highly figurative language.

Link to Christ

In one of his visions, Daniel sees a figure 'like a son of man' who many Christians regard as Christ. In teaching about his second coming, Jesus applied Daniel's image to himself. Christ often preferred to use the title 'son of man' rather than 'son of God' although 'son of man' means little more than 'myself as a person'.

So what's the message?

The primary message of Daniel is 'keep the faith despite provocation'. Daniel refused the royal food (to distance himself from a godless regime), and continued praying – without knowing in advance that the lions would turn their noses up at the lean vegetarian. There are some things in life more important than saving your own skin.

And God is ultimately guiding world events and the course of history. Some might say that he seems to be making a worse job of it than the

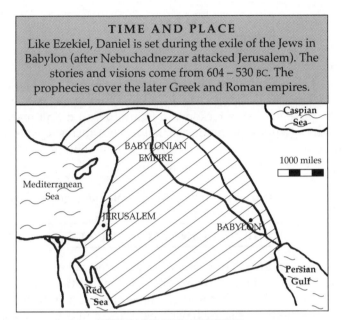

Caspian Sea

BABYLONIAN EMPIRE

1000 miles

Mediterranean Sea

JERUSALEM

BABYLON

Persian Gulf

Red Sea

THE BABYLONIAN EMPIRE

politicians, but Daniel would respond that God's purposes are eternal. The sordid affairs of power-mad nations will be sorted out to the ultimate good of God's people. He's not forgotten you, the prophet is saying, so don't you go forgetting him.

Key verse

Then king Darius wrote to all the nations and peoples of every language throughout the land:… 'For he is the living God and he endures for ever; his kingdom will not be destroyed, his dominion will never end.'

Daniel 6:25, 26

HOSEA

Overview

The story of Hosea could be a bit near the bone for up to a half of British families. Hosea was delighted when God told him to marry a lady called Gomer (because you were reckoned a failure if you didn't marry). They had 3 children (with unpronouncable names) but then she walked out on him and became a tart. Hosea was madly in love with her, so he went to the pimp and greased his palm to get her back. What's more, she came back.

And that, God said, is a parable. My people have gone off with other

---

TOP PERSONALITY – HOSEA

Hosea showed love that went way beyond the call of duty. Hosea not only had the right to divorce his wife, he had the right to have her put to death, for becoming a prostitute. Not only that, but Hosea was taking a risk by having her back, and could have been cast out of society for doing the opposite of what was expected.

---

lovers (gods), but I love them to bits and I'll bring them back.

Link to Christ

There is a parallel between the story of Hosea and Christ's death. That too is a supreme act of self-sacrificing love beyond the call of duty. The Bible uses the idea of 'redemption' (buying back) to describe God's reconciliation of people to himself.

So what's the message?

God will go to enormous lengths to bring people back to faith in himself, and he never stops loving them even when they stop loving him. He even loves them when they walk out on him. That, in fact, is the entire message of the Bible in a nutshell.

So it's probably worth asking what it is that the Gomers of this world (who include each and every one of us) see in other spiritual 'lovers' – the idols we turn to, to give us meaning, purpose, identity and fulfilment. They don't have to be totem poles, Shinto shrines, carefully chosen crystals or feng shui designs. They are usually money, sex and power, in

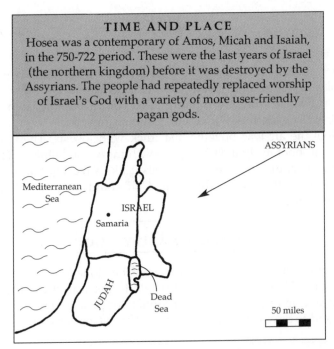

ASSYRIA THREATENS ISRAEL

various disguises. But in the end their promise remains unfulfilled because they leave us wanting more. They stimulate our spiritual appetite rather than feed it. God, it seems, isn't satisfied until we are.

Key verse

> The Lord said to me, 'Go, show your love to your wife again, though she is loved by another and is an adulteress. Love her as the Lord loves the Israelites, though they turn to other gods and love the sacred raisin cakes .'
>
> [Raisin cakes were offered to Baal at harvest time].
>
> Hosea 3:1

JOEL

Overview

The other night half my lawn gave birth to countless sawflies emerging from holes in the ground where they had incubated. The other half had already acted as a womb for mining bees. Fortunately the lawn is small, so the air was never thick with them, just buzzing.

For Joel the air was buzzing *and* thick with locusts. They devoured every green shoot in sight, leaving people hungry and helpless. This short book takes a natural disaster and shines it like a red light at a stream of traffic going in the wrong direction. God could do something worse, unless Judah mends its ways.

TOP PERSONALITY – GOD

It's about time God got a look in (and he alone knows who Joel was, too). There's a touching flip side to the warnings of judgement as God calls, through the prophet, for people to turn back to him and to be assured of forgiveness. That's God for you.

Link to Christ

Despite its mystery and brevity, the book of Joel gets pride of place on the day of Pentecost, when the Holy Spirit (promised by Jesus) filled the first Christians with new life and power. Joel forecast the strange happenings (which were misinterpreted as a drunken party at the time), Peter claimed.

So what's the message?

Natural disasters are not always God's warning shots across errant human brows, but this one was and maybe that's no bad thing. We need the reminder of life's frailty and spiritual dimensions even if we don't like it. It was a bit like a building accident reported once to Jesus; he said that the people who died were no more deserving of death than anyone else, but, he added, turn back to God 'before something worse happens to you'.

Here, as (almost) always in the Bible, judgement is tempered with mercy. We often miss this. While the locusts get everyone hopping mad, God is saying 'now's your chance to turn back to me, and the worse things you actually deserve won't happen.' The New Testament puts it

Locust swarms are frequent and unpredictable throughout the Near East. They are carried on winds, turning the sky dark and filling the air with noise from their beating wings. Their jaws munch through vegetation and they can destroy crops like vines, figs and cornfields very rapidly.

A LOCUST

even more positively; turn back to God and you get the free gift of eternal life thrown in. What could be fairer than that?

Key verse

Return to the Lord your God, for he is gracious and compassionate, slow to anger and abounding in love, and he relents from sending calamity.

Joel 2:13

AMOS

Overview

Don't open this book until after the 9.00 p.m. TV watershed, and prepare yourself for some strong language and horrific scenes. Rich women dripping with jewels and soaked in liquor are harangued as overweight cows. Law lords are being bribed, so poor people could not get justice. Rich landowners force compulsory purchase orders on neighbouring smallholders. Traders rig their scales. Indulgence rules. Life is a party for those who can afford it. The churches are full – of hypocrites.

TOP PERSONALITY – AMOS

Amos was a country bumpkin from Judah. God called him while he was minding sheep and tending sycamore-figs. God told him to take a message of judgement to the Israelites. They told him to return to his former occupation, but he stubbornly refused. In fact, that's all we know about him. He was more interested in God than himself.

Amos reckons there is something wrong, somewhere – and he boldly says so. And suggests that God was calling time.

Link to Christ

There's been a debate for years about whether private failings have any bearing on public life, or whether personal religion should influence public affairs. Amos said public and private are inextricably linked. So did Jesus, even though Jesus majored on the private and Amos on the public.

So what's the message?

To put it bluntly, 'be sure your sins will find you out'. You can't expect God to smile sweetly on you at the pearly gates and welcome you with open arms just because you made a mint and gave some of it to charity. He wants to know how you made it, who you cheated along the way (including your partner) and what you were thinking in church ('what a good boy am I' is not regarded as an appropriate sentiment).

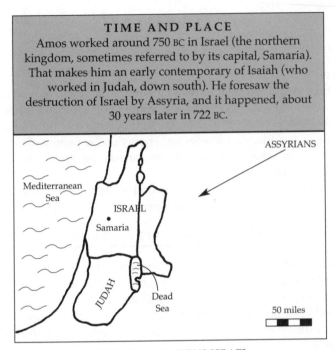

ASSYRIA THREATENS ISRAEL

In the context of Amos, a society in which it is everyone for himself is a society that's built on sand. It can't last, and the fact that it lasts longer than it ought is merely evidence of God's patience, not his approval. It will fall under the weight of its own injustice.

Key verse

Hate evil, love good; maintain justice in the courts. Perhaps the Lord Almighty will have mercy on the remnant of Joseph.
                                                                            Amos 5:15

OBADIAH

Overview

It won't take you any longer to read Obadiah than it will to read these two pages about it – it's the shortest book in the Old Testament (although not the shortest in the whole Bible). Its content is relatively unusual although not unique. It is addressed to a sworn enemy of the people of God, Edom. The book warns Edom that it will pay for having oppressed Israel and Judah over the centuries.

What it's done to others, God says, will be done to it. It doesn't matter that the perpetrators of much of the oppression are long in their graves –

TOP PERSONALITY – ESAU

Anti-heroes have their place in fiction and folklore and this one is Esau, the founder of Edom, whose name is used as a synonym for that nation. He was the son of Isaac and brother of Jacob. Jacob cheated Esau out of his birthright (back in Genesis) mainly because Esau despised it himself. Hatred seems to have been passed on in his genes.

```
                    Isaac
             ┌────────┴────────┐
           Esau              Jacob
             │                  │
         Edomites          Israelites
```

---

history will give its verdict and justice will be seen to have been done.

Link to Christ

The New Testament portrays Jesus as the judge of all nations. He's not just interested in the holy huddles who gather in his name, but in the whole world (which goes its own way and sometimes does unpleasant things to holy huddles).

So what's the message?

The Jews had a tendency to think that God was residing in the temple in Jerusalem. The message here is that God is in foreign countries just as much as in Jerusalem, and he could guide the decisions of foreign rulers just as easily as he could guide his own people. That was comforting, especially when the Jews were depressed and far from home.

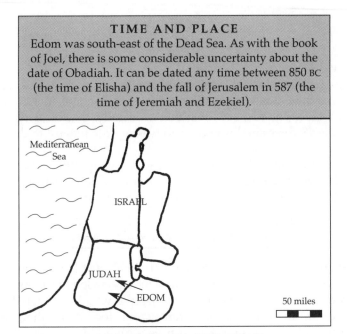

Mediterranean Sea

ISRAEL

JUDAH

EDOM

50 miles

EDOM OFTEN ATTACKED JUDAH

The other part of the message is that God himself will wreak vengeance on our enemies. That's encouraging (unless you're the enemy), because often we're helpless in the face of violence and injustice. It's also fair, because frankly, if we were to do it ourselves we'd give a heck of a lot more than an eye for an eye. Which isn't fair. Think about that next time your blood boils.

Key verse

The day of the Lord is near for all nations. As you have done, it will be done to you; your deeds will return upon your own head.
Obadiah 15

JONAH

Overview

This is the familiar story of Jonah being swallowed by the whale, but there is more to it than that. For one thing no-one (except book illustrators) said it was a whale. The text says 'big fish'. Secondly, that incident occupies just 2 of the 48 verses in this book, and was of little interest to the original author.

What did interest him is that Jonah was a naughty boy. He was told to preach repentance to Nineveh, but went on holiday instead. In the ensuing battle of wills, God's will proved to be the stronger.

TOP PERSONALITY – JONAH

The attractive thing about Jonah is that he's just like us. He does his own thing, is never satisfied, and moans at God for doing what God does best, which is loving the people who Jonah hated. But he's disarmingly honest and transparent, too. When the superstitious sailors conclude the storm is a divine displeasure, Jonah owns up at once to being guilty of annoying God. No 'What me, Sir?' about him.

Link to Christ

Jonah's experience was used by Jesus as a parallel or illustration of his own ultimate fate of crucifixion and resurrection. 'As Jonah was in the fish for three days, so the son of man will be in the ground for three days and then raised to life,' Jesus predicted.

So what's the message?

The primary purpose of this book was to broaden the horizons of the original readers. They'd got a bit parochial as far as God was concerned. They considered he was their God and no-one else's. Jonah was told to preach the same message to Assyria as he was preached to Israel and Judah. This proved that God's interests extend across the world to all peoples equally. What's more, Assyria was Israel's arch enemy. In fact Assyria destroyed Israel in 722 BC. As Jesus said, 'Love your enemies.'...

A secondary message is that when God tells us to do something, even though it seems daft (like loving your enemy), we ought to obey him and

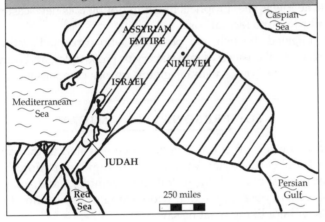

ASSYRIAN EMPIRE SHOWING NINEVEH

not excuse ourselves. If God doesn't know what's what, then no-one does. And if he does, then maybe we ought to listen.

And another lesson is that God doesn't take our no for an answer. If he wants us to do something, he's quite capable of organising a storm here and there to blow us back on course. If we did what he said first time, we could have avoided the discomfort.

Key verse

What I have vowed I will make good. Salvation comes from the Lord.
God speaking to Jonah, Jonah 2:9

MICAH

Overview

Corruption in high places (and low dives) keeps the news media in business, and decent ordinary people in despair. But it's nothing new. In Micah's time it was rife. Prophets like him doubled as newscasters to give gossip and rumour a factual basis.

Micah targeted the rich and powerful who corrupted justice like the Mafia, forced small businesses into slavery or bankruptcy, and compulsorily purchased peasant homes without giving proper compensation. He saves

---

TOP PERSONALITY – MICAH

Micah is the second country yokel to be elevated to the ranks of Minor Prophet (the other was Amos). He came from Moresheth in the south-west of Judah (near Philistine country) and displayed all the powers of observation of a wide-eyed farmer walking the city streets and not liking what he saw.

---

his greatest anger for the religious leaders who were pawns of the rich instead of champions of the poor.

Link to Christ

The book of Micah gets quoted at Christmas carol services because he prophesied that the Messiah would be born in the little town of Bethlehem. In fact, he was simply saying that a great leader will be born in David's family line, which happened to hail from Bethlehem. But the genius of biblical prophecy is that it looks in two directions at once, commenting on past events and predicting future trends.

So what's the message?

Micah, like most other prophets, is passionate about God's righteousness – right thinking expressed by right acting. The people say they want to be about God's business, but they don't match up. They neither think nor act in right ways. Micah took a swipe at the abuses and corruptions, and told them God was not pleased. In fact, if they didn't sort themselves out God

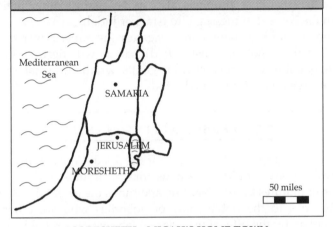

MORESHETH – MICAH'S HOME TOWN

would chase them out of the land (just as Micah no doubt once chased scrumpers out of his farm fields with a pitchfork).

If you want a neat, short summary of what the prophets generally taught, Micah is a good place to start. It's the same message as his contemporaries preached (in fact he uses the same words as Isaiah in one place – but copyright law was looser in those days).

Key verse

He will teach us his ways, so that we may walk in his paths.
Micah 4:2

NAHUM

Overview

Nahum is almost unique in the Bible (and only Jonah comes really close) in addressing his message to Nineveh (in Assyria), the nation which destroyed Israel. Other prophets also spoke against other nations, but always in the context of messages to Israel or Judah.

Nahum pronounces God's anger against the superpower of Assyria. He predicts that another (unspecified) nation will destroy it. Nahum offers no possibility of escape from God's wrath (unusual in the Old Testament). Assyria's time is up. Period.

TOP PERSONALITY – NAHUM

Back in the hippy go lucky days of the 1960s Andy Warhol said that everybody would be famous for 15 minutes. It'll take you about 15 minutes to read Nahum, and that's the extent of his fame. He belongs to the noble army of nobodies who are otherwise overlooked by the official historians. Nahum was probably a Very Nice Man who did a lot of Good Work, but only God knows what it was, and he decided not to tell us.

Link to Christ

Like Nahum, Christ also predicted the downfall of nations who opposed God and God's people. Christ was also the champion of the underdog, and perhaps would have called Nahum to be an apostle, had he lived 650 years later.

So what's the message?

Fire and brimstone. Nahum's catch-phrase is meant to make us shudder: 'I (God) am against you.' In the book of Jonah, Nineveh was given (and took) a chance to repent from its bad ways. In Nahum, no such offer is made. Things have gone too far. There is no hope. The only uncertainty is *when* the city (and nation) will fall, not if.

That's scary. It reminds all generations that God isn't a big sugar daddy in the sky who gets a bit cross now and then with people's shortcomings but is generally able to forgive them after he's thrown the odd tantrum.

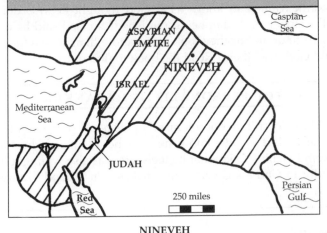

NINEVEH

He's the real God of justice who is extremely patient, but who in the end will throw the book at those who insist on putting him out of their lives. Those who oppose God's people will suffer because it's the same as opposing God.

Key verse

He cares for those who trust him, but with an overwhelming flood...he will pursue his foes into darkness.

Nahum 1:7,8

HABAKKUK

Overview

Just to prove that the Bible doesn't entirely preach to the converted, meet Habakkuk, the Man with Questions. God has never been easy to understand (not least because he's invisible) and you have to feel some sympathy for the perpetual agnostics who agonise over their angst.

Habakkuk wanted to know what God thought he was doing. Why weren't the sinners in Judah being punished? So God said he'd send the Babylonians to do it. But they took rather more than an eye for an eye, so how could God 'use' them? Read the book to find out...

TOP PERSONALITY – HABAKKUK

Habakkuk doesn't mention himself in his book, so we don't know who he is. But we do know he's an honest man who has no problem in telling God what he feels. He was also willing to listen carefully to God's answers. That makes him a good example to follow.

Link to Christ

Habakkuk was a doubter, a bit like Thomas in the New Testament. Thomas, the apostle, was out when Jesus called after his resurrection and refused to believe that Jesus had risen from the dead, until he had some proof. Jesus sorted him out, but mildly rebuked him when he said 'blessed are those who believe and have *not* seen'. Jesus understands doubt, but it's got to be real, and not a weak excuse for not believing.

So what's the message?

Habakkuk believes passionately in God's holiness and essential goodness. He could not understand why God seemed to tolerate the sins of his hypocritical contemporaries for so long. And then he could not understand God's punishment when it did finally come. The Babylonian war machine trampled the Judeans into the dust. The innocents perished with the guilty. The punishment seemed much greater than the crime.

The answer given to Habakkuk is that God *is* holy, that his concerns are global and long term. All perpetrators of injustice (including the

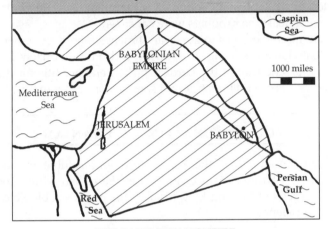

THE BABYLONIAN EMPIRE

Babylonians, *even though God uses them for a short term purpose*) will be judged accordingly. The message is: be patient, and trust God. Doubt would be easier.

Key verse

Though the olive crop fails and the fields produce no food...yet I will rejoice in the Lord, I will be joyful in God my Saviour.
Habakkuk 3:17,18

ZEPHANIAH

Overview

Reading the minor prophets one after the other can get a bit tedious. You're really meant to read them in the context of the books of Kings and Chronicles. So if Zephaniah sounds a bit familiar, console yourself with the fact that at least the prophets were consistent.

Here are more messages to the errant Judeans (and a few other nations) with the Babylonians stirring up a dust cloud on the horizon. Zephaniah makes a lot of 'the Day of the Lord', which is another title for the day of reckoning. This is careful literature, not spontaneous outpourings.

TOP PERSONALITY – ZEPHANIAH

Zephaniah is another of the Almost Anonymous Bible writers. He tells us he's a descendant of good king Hezekiah, which means he's also related to good king Josiah. This guy's got blue blood – and a conscience, too.

Link to Christ

Zephaniah predicted the destruction of Jerusalem, and looked forward to the restoration of Jerusalem after its (still-future, to Zephaniah) destruction by the Babylonians, which happened in 587 BC. Christ also predicted the destruction of Jerusalem, or at least of its temple (the symbol of God's presence among his people). The temple in Jerusalem was indeed destroyed by the Romans in AD 70, and has never been re-built.

So what's the message?

The people of Judah should have obeyed God, but have not done so, and must therefore face the consequences. Zephaniah fortells the 'Day of the Lord', when judgement will come to the surrounding tribes who have oppressed Israel and Judah, and predicts the fall and rise of Jerusalem itself.

Writing in poetry rather than prose, the prophet gives graphic descriptions of 'the Day of the Lord'. When Jerusalem did fall, it was indeed 'a day of darkness and gloom' in the emotional and political sense, as

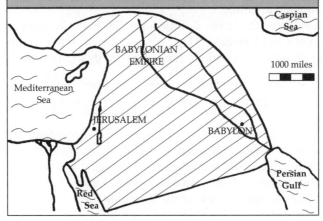

**THE BABYLONIAN EMPIRE TOOK OVER FROM THE
ASSYRIAN EMPIRE IN 612 BC**

Nebuchadnezzar lit the blue touch paper and watched the smoke rise.
You'll find similar language in the New Testament relating to another
'Day of the Lord', the return of Christ and the end of the world. This is a
sober reminder that history can repeat itself, and we ought to take the
possibility of God's judgement seriously.

Key verse

*Seek righteousness, seek humility; perhaps you will be sheltered on the
day of the Lord's anger.*

Zephaniah 2:3

HAGGAI

Overview

Once upon a time management theory said that to get the best out of your workers, you whipped them. Today, the fashion is to gee them up, like a sluggish racehorse that doesn't fancy jumping Beechers Brook during the Grand National at Aintree.

You can't blame the horse. But the jump has got to be jumped, not least because there's 100-1 at stake. Haggai is a jockey trying to get the sluggish Judeans to rebuild the temple in Jerusalem. To them, it's a big hurdle and

---

TOP PERSONALITY – HAGGAI

Haggai was a contemporary of the prophet Zechariah, and they both had a similar message. A while later, Ezra returned to Jerusalem and worked with Nehemiah. Haggai was a team player, speaking his lines clearly. That's quite common in the Bible, and meant to be a characteristic of the Christian life.

---

they haven't the confidence to try it. But there's a lot at stake, he says: like God's honour, and their future.

Link to Christ

The temple under construction is 'the second temple' (Solomon's was the first). By the time of Jesus, it too had been destroyed (by the Roman general Pompey) and Herod the Great had built a more splendid one. But Jesus said it would be temporary, and that true worship couldn't be focused on a building. (See Temple time-line in 2 Chronicles on page 37.)

So what's the message?

Basically, get your priorities right. (Which we've heard before, and will hear again). The people have not been idle in the 16 years since they trekked back from Babylon. They've planted crops and built their own houses, but God's house – the symbol of his presence – lies in ruins. 'Who matters most?' asks Haggai 'you or God?'.

Haggai points to 'signs' which they've missed. Life hasn't been easy. Crops have failed. They've struggled to make ends meet. In all that time,

TIME AND PLACE
We're back in Jerusalem after the exile in Babylon. The
last exiles were taken away by Nebuchadnezzar in 587
BC, and some returned in 536 BC. They planned to rebuild
the temple as their first task, but it was too much – so
they stopped. Haggai leaps into the saddle in
520 BC and encouraged them to finish it by 515 BC.

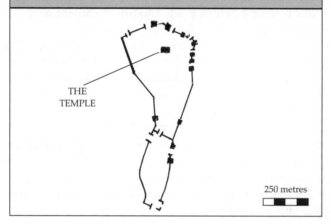

THE
TEMPLE

250 metres

THE TEMPLE AREA IN JERUSALEM

their faith has been nominal rather than vital. Haggai says they should
have turned back to God whole-heartedly when things first started going
wrong. That's often the paradox of Christian living. Things only start to
improve when we put God first.

Key verse

*Is it time for you to be living in your panelled houses, while (God's)
house remains a ruin?*

Haggai 1:4

ZECHARIAH

Overview

Zechariah said the same thing to the same people as Haggai. Yet this book couldn't be more different. With Zechariah, we enter once more the dreamscape of visionaries. We see weird and wonderful sights infused with symbolic meaning, which poets and artists can appreciate more than those who see prophecies as equations to be solved.

There are two sections to this book and no-one can agree whether they were both by the same person. Chapters 1-8 are to inspire the returned exiles to rebuild the temple, as Haggai also sought to do. Chapters 9-14

TOP PERSONALITY

Zechariah was a priest, probably born in Babylon, but returned with his parents as a child to Jerusalem in the first wave of hopefuls in 536 BC. He obviously had a vivid imagination (or else he ate too much cheese before going to bed), but his dreams are symbolic rather than bizarre.

---

look further into the future and are vaguer pictures of God's ultimate victory.

Link to Christ

There are several 'messianic' passages in this book which are quoted in the New Testament as relating to Christ. One (in chapter 9) relates to Christ's 'triumphal entry' into Jerusalem on Palm Sunday, riding on a donkey which trod on people's jackets laid down as a makeshift red carpet, while bystanders vandalised the palm trees to create flags.

So what's the message?

Primarily, this is a message of encouragement. God speaks through the images of the first eight chapters to reassure his oppressed people that the temple will be rebuilt and that God's people will be protected by his 'wall of fire' (his holiness). The small beginnings are not to be despised. Just like the the feeding of the 5000, God can do a lot with a little.

And that's a message everyone needs to hear. If you're concerned for God and for goodness, you can get pretty low when he's despised and

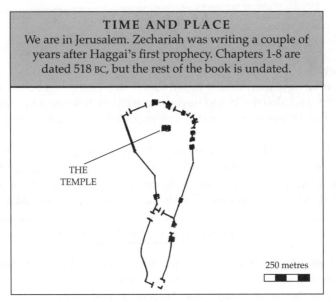

TIME AND PLACE
We are in Jerusalem. Zechariah was writing a couple of
years after Haggai's first prophecy. Chapters 1-8 are
dated 518 BC, but the rest of the book is undated.

THE
TEMPLE

250 metres

THE TEMPLE AREA IN JERUSALEM

evil seems to be let loose. You wonder if your little bit is achieving very
much, but Zechariah says it's important. He also reminds Joshua (the high
priest of the time) that he can't rely on his office to keep him right with
God. Clerics are human too and need the same spiritual renewal as the
rest of us.

Key verse

Who despises the day of small things?

Zechariah 4:10

MALACHI

Overview

Well, you've now reached the top of the 39 steps – the last book in the Old Testament, and also the last to have been written. It's also a bit like the last item on the TV news: reasonably upbeat but with a serious point tucked inside.

The book of Malachi addressed the prosperous people who were getting spiritually complacent. They were expecting the day of the Lord (by now a familiar Old Testament theme) which they thought would be a triumphal victory of God over his enemies. Watch out, says Malachi, it is

---

TOP PERSONALITY – MALACHI

Note that Malachi is *not* to be pronounced *malarky* (as in messing about) but some scholars do reckon someone's having us on here, because 'Malachi' means 'my messenger' and could just be a *nom de plume*. So what's wrong with being faithful to God and not letting anyone know who you are? Fits the message, anyway. He's a practising preacher.

---

coming but you'll get your fingers burned as well if you're not careful.

Link to Christ

Malachi predicted the prophet Elijah would return before 'the day of the Lord'. Jesus interpreted his own advent as 'the day of the Lord' and said John had come in the 'spirit and power' of Elijah to prepare the way.

So what's the message?

Don't give up being faithful to God when times are easy, life is good, the sun's shining and you're doing very nicely, thank-you. If anyone out there has ever experienced such a rare phenomenon, donations to the author's benevolent fund will be greatly appreciated. But you'd better make some donations to charity and the church first, because Malachi reckons that God's blessing dwindles when the offertory plate is half empty.

Not that God is money-grabbing, but because generosity to God and to others is a sign that we're prepared to put God first, and when we really are prepared to put God first, then he can bless us real good, as the

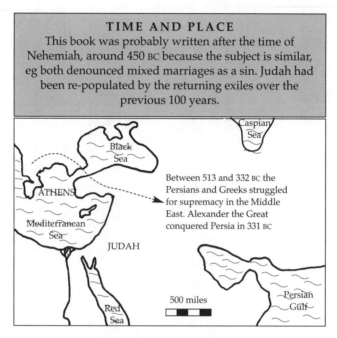

Caspian
Sea

Black
Sea

ATHENS

Between 513 and 332 BC the
Persians and Greeks struggled
for supremacy in the Middle
East. Alexander the Great
conquered Persia in 331 BC

Mediterranean
Sea

JUDAH

500 miles

Persian
Gulf

Red
Sea

JUDAH IN INTER-TESTAMENT TIMES

Americans say unfortunately and ungrammatically. Furthermore, peaceful
times are opportunities for service, not for indulgence, for mission and
not for retrenchment. So let's go!

Key verse

*Have we not all one Father? Did not one God create us? Why do we
profane the covenant of our ancestors by breaking faith with one
another?*

Malachi 2:10

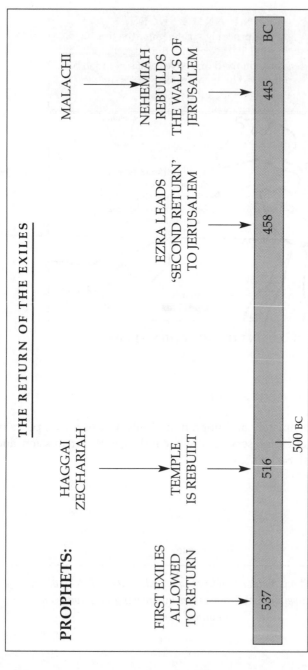

THE RETURN OF THE EXILES

PROPHETS:

			HAGGAI ZECHARIAH	EZRA LEADS 'SECOND RETURN' TO JERUSALEM	MALACHI

FIRST EXILES ALLOWED TO RETURN → 537

TEMPLE IS REBUILT → 516

500 BC

EZRA LEADS 'SECOND RETURN' TO JERUSALEM → 458

NEHEMIAH REBUILDS THE WALLS OF JERUSALEM → 445

BC

The exile lasted 70 years, from the first exiles being taken in 604 BC (including Daniel and Ezekiel) to the first return in 537 BC. After Malachi, the prophets were silent for over 400 years (the 'intertestamental period') until John the Baptist

THE NEW TESTAMENT

MATTHEW

Overview

Matthew is the first of the 4 Gospels (although it was not the first to be written – that was Mark). Each Gospel gives an account of the life of Christ. 'Gospel' means 'good news'. If you've been plodding steadily through the Bible from the beginning, here's some other good news: you've now read 60% of the whole Bible. The gospel of Matthew gets off to a bad start: a genealogy and a long list of names, to show Christ's ancestry. Family history has its place. Matthew is the most Jewish of the 4 gospels, with many Old Testament quotes, because the author wants to

---

TOP PERSONALITY – MATTHEW

Matthew (also called Levi in the gospel, no relation to Jeans) is the forerunner of Shakespeare's Shylock: a Jewish money maker who collects taxes for the Romans and charges taxpayers over the odds. He gives it all up to follow Jesus. Matthew is not the first or last to discover that money can't buy love.

---

show that Jesus was the promised Messiah. Matthew focuses on Christ as a teacher and preacher.

Christ as Messiah

Matthew's keen on the fact that Jesus was the Messiah, the expected King, who had been predicted by the prophets. What happens in the story, he says, is no accident. God planned it all in advance. Therefore, he implies, we can have confidence in both the story and the person it points to.

So what's the message?

Matthew shoots the image of 'gentle Jesus meek and mild' out of the sky. After recounting the infant Jesus' near-death experience Matthew immediately bashes us with the 'Sermon on the Mount.' People who simply applaud this teaching as a great ideal shouldn't be believed. It's not simply an 'ideal'; it's *the* deal, the one we are meant to accept.

The fact is, turning the other cheek, being God-centred, not thinking about where your next crust is coming from, and being critical of ourselves before others (and taking the 'critical planks' out of our own

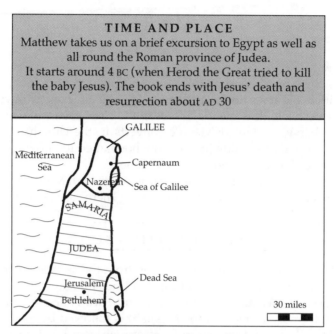

GALILEE

Mediterranean
Sea

Capernaum

Nazareth

Sea of Galilee

SAMARIA

JUDEA

Jerusalem

Bethlehem

Dead Sea

30 miles

THE ROMAN PROVINCE OF JUDEA

eyes, before criticising the 'specks' in other people's, as Jesus put it) are
about the most difficult things in life.

The really awesome thing is that the book *starts* with Jesus' secret of
happiness (the Beatitudes) which turn all our values on their heads. This
isn't a religion for other-worldly wimps and monks. It's for hard-nosed
tax inspectors (and everyone else who makes money or dreams of it). It is
for people in the real world who want more than a surface experience of
life. If we don't follow it, we're lost. Help!

Key verse

*Enter through the narrow gate. For wide is the gate and broad is the
road that leads to destruction, and many enter through it. But small
is the gate and narrow is the road that leads to life, and only a few
find it.*

Matthew 7:13,14

MARK

Overview

If you've never read a Gospel, this is the best place to start. It was the first to be written and it's a no-frills account of the life of Jesus, with very little comment or theological agenda. It tells of the basic events of Christ's life. It was probably written for Gentile converts in the church of Rome or enquirers who lived outside Judea and who wanted to know more about who this Jesus had been, and what he'd done.

Mark's gospel was copied almost verbatim by both Matthew and Luke who then added their own material to it. There is just one unsolved

---

TOP PERSONALITY – PETER

Mark derived most of his information from the apostle Peter, but Mark does not censor the bad bits, and he still shows Peter (the disciples' spokesman with the big mouth) warts and all. Peter's triumph (recognising Jesus as Messiah) is followed by his failure (advising Jesus on how not to be a Messiah) and his despair (his famous cowardly triple denial of Jesus). Some team leader. Yet Peter was nick-named the 'Rock' by Jesus, who said 'On this rock I will build my church'. The church is for ordinary failures like you and me.

---

mystery in it: how did Mark end it? The final chapter seems to have been lost on the cutting room floor and attempts to recover it have proved unsatisfactory.

Christ as Healer

The opening words tell us the book is 'the Gospel of Jesus Christ, the Son of God.' Mark shows Jesus teaching and doing things that revealed him to be the Messiah, but also shows that Jesus didn't go around shouting 'I'm the Messiah'. This man behaved like a Son of God should.

So what's the message?

Controversy dogged Jesus' footsteps from day one. He broke all the laws of public relations: he got people's backs up. There's a fun story in chapter two about a paralysed man being lowered through the ceiling so Jesus

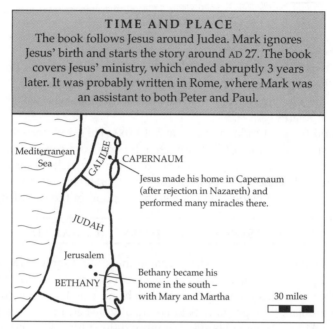

Mediterranean Sea

GALILEE

CAPERNAUM

Jesus made his home in Capernaum (after rejection in Nazareth) and performed many miracles there.

JUDAH

Jerusalem

BETHANY

Bethany became his home in the south – with Mary and Martha

30 miles

THE MINISTRY OF JESUS

could heal him (fun to read; the poor man must have been terrified). And what did Jesus do? Forgave his sins, then healed him as an afterthought. Only God could forgive sins. The religious authorities got the point, but wouldn't accept the claim.

Then there's a scrap about Jewish rules of uncleanness. Jesus says pointedly that it's your dirty thoughts not your religious habits that are really unclean. In the end, they can't stand him any longer and do away with him. The fact is, Mark says, he was born to die: not in a fatalistic way, but in a purposeful way. God did not shield his Son from suffering and misunderstanding, but used it to further his purposes for humankind.

Key verse

> *Whoever wants to be great among you must be your servant, and whoever wants to be first must be slave of all. For even the Son of Man did not come to be served, but to serve, and to give his life as a ransom for all.*
> Jesus speaking to his disciples, Mark 10:43,44

LUKE

Overview

Luke's Gospel is a carefully researched account of Jesus' life. Luke alone gives us the birth narratives of Jesus and gives a lot of space to the last week of Jesus's life. He wrote it for a man called 'Theophilus', who was probably a Gentile Christian.

It would be good to know more about Luke. He's an interesting person who appears in the story of the early church (Acts) as a companion of Paul. Paul describes Luke as a doctor. Unlike some of the quacks of his day, Luke seems genuinely concerned for humanity in general. His two books (he also wrote Acts) show considerable interest in the poor, in the disabled, and in

---

TOP PERSONALITY – JOHN THE BAPTIST

John the Baptist, Jesus' cousin, prepared the ground for Jesus by calling people to turn back to God. He lived as a desert hermit (like Elijah to whom he was compared). Like Elijah, he was hated by rulers. Unlike Elijah, they got him. Salome literally dished up his head for Herod Antipas' dinner because her mum did not like John's criticism of her marriage. Luke omits this last fact, but apart from that Luke gives more space to John the Baptist than the other gospels.

---

women. (As a pastor, you understand, not as a philanderer. Women usually had a raw deal in those days.)

Christ as Man

Jesus is shown pre-eminently as a person with great human compassion. He stops and talks to an old woman who pours out her problems when Jesus is hurrying somewhere else; he invites himself to tea at Zacchaeus' house when most 'respectable' people would have bombed it; he told the story about the prodigal son, the renegade who is welcomed back home by his dad. In fact, Luke makes Jesus believable – and attractive.

So what's the message?

Luke has several incidents that are unique to his Gospel. One is the encounter of a couple on the Emmaus road with the risen Jesus, who teaches them and then reveals himself to them. And earlier, Jesus commissioned 70 disciples (in addition to the original 12) to extend his mission and message.

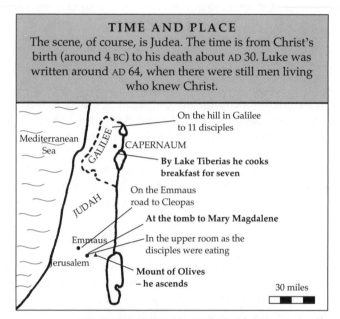

On the hill in Galilee
to 11 disciples

Mediterranean
Sea

CAPERNAUM

GALILEE

By Lake Tiberias he cooks
breakfast for seven

JUDAH

On the Emmaus
road to Cleopas

At the tomb to Mary Magdalene

Emmaus

In the upper room as the
disciples were eating

Jerusalem

Mount of Olives
– he ascends

30 miles

THE RESURRECTION APPEARANCES

Luke implies that Jesus' message is for ordinary people puzzled by life's enigmas. Luke also shows that Jesus wants those who embrace that message to share it with others, a theme he develops further in his second book – the Acts of the Apostles.

Christianity isn't simply a matter of private beliefs, but also of public affirmation of them. Nor is it just one option among a variety of philosophies. This is God's revelation to the world, and therefore is to be shared with the world. After all, you'd share your chocolates with a friend, wouldn't you?

Key verse

'This is the one about whom it is written. "I will send my messenger ahead of you, who will prepare the way for you." I tell you, among those born of woman there is no-one greater than John; yet the one who is least in the kingdom of God is greater than he.'
Jesus, referring to John the Baptist, Luke 7:27,28

JOHN

Overview
And now for something completely different. St John's Gospel is not like the others. It covers the life of Christ but it doesn't tell the half. John isn't bothered about what happened so much as why it happened and what it meant.

If you want to know what it means to know God personally, then John speaks your language. If you want to find out how the disciples came to understand who Jesus was (God in human form) and what was his

---

TOP PERSONALITY – JESUS

Jesus the good shepherd. Jesus who turns the tables in the temple, chats up a woman who's had more partners than Elizabeth Taylor, who confounds his critics, heals the sick, raises the dead, enjoys his food, cries his eyes out, lets himself be killed, forgives his killers and rises from the dead. Awesome.

---

essential mission (to bring us to know God), look no further; John is full of it. It is also eminently quotable.

Christ as God
John's essential message is that Jesus is the way to God, the truth about God, and that he gives the life of God to ordinary people. He includes 7 great 'I AM' sayings (I am the bread of life, I am the light of the world, I am the gate for the sheep, I am the good shepherd, I am the resurrection, I am the way, the truth and the life, I am the vine) which together with the straight claim to divinity in 8:58 ('before Abraham was born, I am') left his hearers in no doubt who he thought he was.

So what's the message?
John brings us to where faith hits the road and either splatters like a squashed hedgehog or speeds on like a Michelin roadhog. Who do you think Jesus is? he's asking his readers. And if he's who I say he is, then what are you going to do about it? You can't be like that woman in John Osbourne's old play *Look back in anger* who, when she's told 'Jesus Christ died for your sins' replies, 'Oh, yes, I heard about that.'

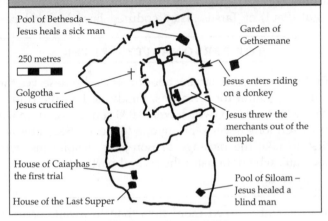

Pool of Bethesda –
Jesus heals a sick man

Garden of
Gethsemane

250 metres

Jesus enters riding
on a donkey

Golgotha –
Jesus crucified

Jesus threw the
merchants out of the
temple

House of Caiaphas –
the first trial

Pool of Siloam –
Jesus healed a
blind man

House of the Last Supper

EVENTS IN JERUSALEM

It's in-your-face stuff. Jesus tells Nicodemus bluntly, 'You must be born again' (which means being completely re-formed in your thinking and feeling and being). After all, if God has visited this planet, you'd be daft not to respond to what he said. If God doesn't know how we're supposed to live, who does?

Key verse

For God so loved the world that he gave his one and only Son, that whoever believes in him shall not perish but have eternal life.
John 3:16

THE ACTS OF THE APOSTLES

Overview

So, your leader is dead and your hopes dashed. Not the best basis for establishing a lasting and influential multi-national movement, is it? But it happened, and this book (written by St Luke) describes how. In the words of their opponents, Jesus' followers 'turned the world upside down' (although they themselves would have said 'right way up').

Following the resurrection of Jesus, hope was restored and new spiritual power received by the apostles who began to gossip the Christian message across the Roman Empire, ably abetted by their star convert Saul (Paul) of Tarsus. They endured hardship and persecution

---

TOP PERSONALITY – PETER

The first part of Acts is largely about Peter, who deserves the top step on the podium for 2 reasons. Firstly he had the courage to preach the first sermon (which won 3,000 converts and unlike one of Paul's sermons never sent anyone to sleep). Secondly he was the first to take the message to non-Jews despite his personal doubts. Paul, who dominates the second part of the book of Acts, later eclipsed him.

---

along the way, and sparked more riots than Millwall soccer club. The church started with a bang.

Link to Christ

Christ only makes 2 brief appearances in the story in Acts. First, at the Ascension (his last resurrection appearance) and then in a special appearance to Saul on the Damascus Road. But the whole story in Acts is the outworking of what Christ had forecast (and what he had prepared his followers for) and shows how Christ affected many people after his death and resurrection.

So what's the message?

You can't keep a good God down. The resurrection of Jesus forms the focal point of the preaching of Peter and Paul (and, presumably, everyone else). By and large, they didn't go around accusing people of nasty sins and threatening them with hell fire (although that did happen on

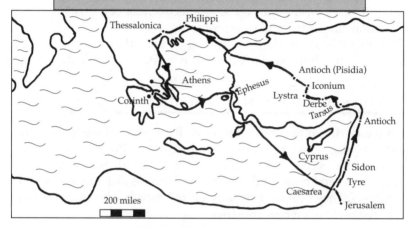

PAUL'S SECOND JOURNEY

occasions, because God is, after all, the eternal Judge) but instead amazed
people by telling them that God was alive and could be known and
experienced through the risen Christ. This was good news indeed to
people who still thought in terms of appeasing the gods with rituals.

Alongside that teaching is the demonstration of spiritual power to
authenticate it, and the book has sometimes been dubbed 'The Acts of the
Holy Spirit'. We can see, as well as hear, that God is active among his people.

Key verse

*After they prayed, the place where they were meeting was shaken. And
they were all filled with the Holy Spirit and spoke the word of God
boldly.*

Acts 4:31

99

PAUL'S LETTER TO THE ROMANS

Overview
If any of Paul's thirteen letters deserve being called his 'magnum opus', it is this. Unlike all but one other (Ephesians), Romans is not a letter dealing with pastoral and theological questions but a carefully-argued treatise (answering the common questions asked by thoughtful Christians of the time). It focuses on the purpose and effectiveness of Christ's death and resurrection, and stresses the need for faith.

Probably it has been the most influential of Paul's letters. St Augustine (a key early-church theologian), the reformer Martin Luther, the evangelist

---

TOP PERSONALITIES – PRISCILLA AND AQUILA

In the credits at the end of his letter, Paul pays tribute to Priscilla and Aquila, who had returned to their native Rome (having fled during an earlier persecution). This husband and wife team appear several times in the New Testament as skilled pastors and teachers. They provided stability for the church when the apostles moved on to plant new churches.

John Wesley, and the modern 'neo-orthodox' theologian Karl Barth were all converted through it. But it's not an easy read.

Link to Christ
This book describes the central purpose of Christ's mission. This is the Bible's longest and most thorough exploration of where the 'sacrifice' of Christ, made through his death and resurrection, fits in with God's plan of 'salvation'. (The jargon is unavoidable; this is a theological treatise).

So what's the message?
It revolves around one statement: the just shall life by faith. If you want to get on the right side of God you've got to do absolutely nothing. On the other hand, you've got to give everything.

Paul explains that every human being is separated from God because of inherent and acquired 'sin' (which means shoving God out of the centre of our lives). Try as we might, we can't 'atone' (make amends) for that. So, while we were helpless, Paul says, Christ died for us. The perfect

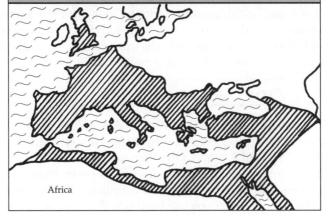

Africa

THE ROMAN EMPIRE

man who was also God brought God and human beings back together, by
suffering in our place the just reward for sin (which happens to be death,
which is separation from God). All we can do is accept that 'by faith'. But
having accepted it, Paul says the only loving response is to give ourselves
as living sacrifices to God's service. 'The entrance fee is nothing, but the
annual subscription is everything'.

Key verse

*All have sinned and fall short of the glory of God, and are justified
freely by his grace through the redemption that came by Christ Jesus.*
Romans 3:23,24

PAUL'S FIRST LETTER TO THE CORINTHIANS

Overview

If Paul's letter to the Romans is sublime, his first letter to the Corinthians is ridiculous. Or at least, the people Paul is writing to are ridiculous, in Christian terms. They claim to honour Christ but they're as competitive as Virgin Atlantic and British Airways (with no love lost between them), and their sexual habits rival those of free-living Hollywood B-movie stars.

In church they're swinging from the chandeliers like extreme Pentecostals, shouting each other down in a medley of garbled prophecies each

---

TOP PERSONALITY – APOLLOS

Apollos was an intellectual Jew from Alexandria who came to Christian faith in Ephesus, through Aquila and Priscilla (mentioned in Paul's letter to the Romans). Apollos subsequently taught and ministered faithfully in Corinth (with about as much effectiveness as Paul). Apollos was a brilliant teacher, but Paul warns the people not to argue about whether Apollos or Paul is the greater, and points them back towards Christ.

---

claiming to be the authentic word of the Lord. Their communion services resemble a teenager's drink and drugs party, making modern church scandals tame by comparison. And so Paul writes to call them to order.

Link to Christ

1 Corinthians describes the church as 'the body of Christ'. This letter portrays a picture of the church, with all its varied gifts and ministries, as a (very imperfect) visible expression of the risen Christ on earth. It is also a metaphor of the essential unity of the church worldwide. Christ is not divided, Paul stresses.

So what's the message?

This letter covers a multitude of sins. You can boil them down to four.

1 Get rid of competitiveness in the church. We're all the same in the bath, and all equal before God. Splitting into rival factions is a contradiction in Christian terms and only leads to tears.

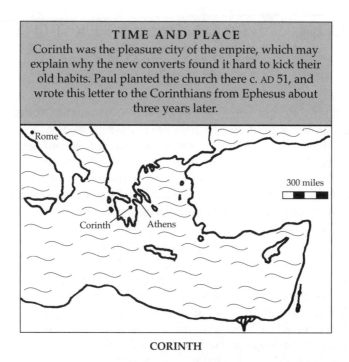

TIME AND PLACE
Corinth was the pleasure city of the empire, which may explain why the new converts found it hard to kick their old habits. Paul planted the church there c. AD 51, and wrote this letter to the Corinthians from Ephesus about three years later.

Rome

300 miles

Corinth   Athens

CORINTH

2 Get rid of immorality. People weren't made as sex machines but as unique beings capable of special and lasting relationships expressed partly (but not exclusively) through sexuality.

3 Think about others, not yourselves. There was genuine confusion over whether Christians ought to eat meat because it had been slaughtered in pagan ceremonies. It's OK to eat it, says Paul, but only if by doing so you don't offend another Christian. Liberty isn't absolute.

4 Christian worship ought to be orderly not chaotic because it is to reflect the God who brings order out of chaos.

Key verse

Love is patient, love is kind. It does not envy, it does not boast, it is not proud. It is not rude, it is not self-seeking, it is not easily angered, it keeps no record of wrongs.

1 Corinthians 13:4,5

PAUL'S SECOND LETTER TO THE CORINTHIANS

Overview

2 Corinthians brings some relief after 1 Corinthians. Although the problems have not gone away (there are still disputes due to rivalry and a new debate about finance), this is a letter of encouragement and reassurance. There can be happy endings when God is honoured.

Actually, this is probably Paul's fourth letter to Corinth. He refers to two others (now lost). The first preceded our 1 Corinthians, and the third came between our 1 and 2 Corinthians. There was a lot of personal contact

---

TOP PERSONALITY – PAUL

In 2 Corinthians Paul bares his heart like in no other letter. He describes the comfort he has received from God in suffering, and then lists the suffering. Paul was no fair-weather preacher. He knew poverty, homelessness and hunger, wrongful imprisonment and lawless muggings. He lived out of a suitcase for years and was not in good health. That's commitment.

---

too, after Paul's first visit to plant the church. Some concerned Corinthians had visited Paul, and Paul's assistants Timothy and Titus visited Corinth. There was one brief 'painful' visit by Paul himself.

Link to Christ

2 Corinthians introduces us to an important (but not often developed) aspect of Christ's ministry: reconciliation. Through his death and resurrection, Jesus reconciled us to God, Paul says, like enemies who have now become friends. Therefore, we too should be reconciled to him and to each other.

So what's the message?

God is good. It's an old message that bears repeating in the context of Paul's catalogue of suffering. Today, we seem to scream at God (and the health service) as soon as we get a pimple on the nose. Paul screamed at God three times over an unspecified 'thorn in the flesh' and then accepted

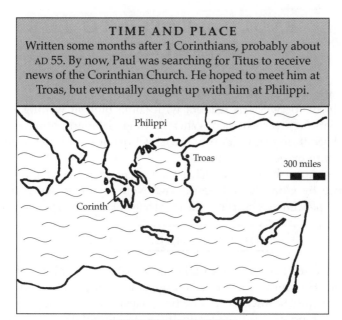

Philippi

Troas

300 miles

Corinth

CORINTH AND PHILIPPI

that being human was by definition to be physically imperfect, and trusted that God could give him strength in his weakness – which he did.

There's a lot about money here, too. Paul encourages generosity not to feather his own nest (he didn't have one) but to support less fortunate Christians who were suffering deprivation. He says that God has been generous to us (he gave his Son) so we ought to reciprocate. And when we give (sacrificially) we are more open to receive God's grace – we are more dependant upon him, which is never a bad thing.

Key verse

> *So [the Lord] said to me, 'My grace is sufficient for you, for my power is made perfect in weakness.' Therefore I will boast all the more gladly about my weaknesses, so that Christ's power may rest on me....For when I am weak, then I am strong.*
>
> 2 Corinthians 12:9,10

PAUL'S LETTER TO THE GALATIANS

Overview

The problem for western readers with some biblical writing is that its Jewish roots are over-exposed. When reading Galatians, you have to shift gear and see it first as written to Jewish Christians, and then translate its concepts into modern equivalents.

Quite simply, the Galatian Christians were abandoning the gospel (of acceptance by God through faith) and were trying to work their own passage to heaven by observing the Jewish law. Paul was appalled, and said

---

TOP PERSONALITY – PAUL

Here we see Paul the multi-talented apostle as the practical theologian. He knows his stuff, he argues it with passion and, most importantly, he reveals its practical relevance. Theology, to Paul, was nothing dry and academic. It was the foundation of an active life.

---

this was 'another gospel'. These people were clearly somewhat assertive; this letter includes Paul's famous contrast of 'works of the lower nature' (sexual immorality, idolatry, hatred, discord, jealousy, fits of rage, selfish ambition, drunkeness, orgies etc) with the 'fruit of the Spirit' (love, joy, peace, patience, kindness, goodness, faithfulness, gentleness and self-control).

Link to Christ

Christ, says Paul, has set us free from the curse of the Old Testament law (a curse because it was incapable of effecting a permanent reconciliation between man and God). Once more he says that faith in the crucified and risen Christ is the only sure way for a person to enter a relationship with God. Then we're free to be the people God intended us to be.

So what's the message?

What idiot said that you could be a Christian by living a good, moral life without also worshipping Christ as Son of God and trusting him alone to get you through the pearly gates? No, I don't know who it was, either, but

that anonymous heretic was the heir of the Galatians who Paul rather unceremoniously called 'fools' and, because of their insistence on Jewish ceremonies, told to go and castrate themselves.

We're back to the Romans thesis, that faith (in the sense of personal trust) is all you need. Here, it's no matter of theory but a matter of life and death. If you reckon you can make your own way, you imply that Christ's death was unnecessary and you're liable to pride. And pride, as everyone knows, leads to a fall from grace. And, Paul adds, you can only produce the 'fruit of the Spirit' (love, joy, peace, patience, kindness, goodness, faithfulness, gentleness and self control) if you draw on the Spirit of Christ.

Key verse

I have been crucified with Christ and I no longer live, but Christ lives in me. The life I live in the body, I live by faith in the Son of God, who loved me and gave himself for me.

Galatians 2:20

PAUL'S LETTER TO THE EPHESIANS

Overview

Now this is a peach of a letter. Like Romans, it's an essay rather than a personal letter. But it's short, wide-ranging, thought-provoking and inspiring. Unfortunately, Paul writes such long sentences that you die of suffocation if you try to read it aloud. (Some versions of the Bible get round it by putting full stops where Paul never intended them.)

But that's because he's excited by God's love, God's forgiveness, the new life God gives to those who trust him, and the practical challenge to

---

TOP PERSONALITY – TYCHICUS

The only person to get a mention is Tychicus, the newscaster of the apostolic church. He carried news about Paul to the churches praying for him, and at the same time found out how the churches were getting on. Even in days of quill pens and pony express, communication was deemed vital.

---

live for Christ in the real world day by day. Even in the heat of spiritual battle with the forces of evil, he says, victory is assured. Give this one some quality time.

Link to Christ

This is one of Paul's great celebrations of the Trinity, displaying the Father, Son and Holy Spirit as a trio playing in complete harmony (not unison). He portrays Christ as the agent of spiritual reconciliation, the head of the church. Christ is the person with whom Christians enjoy a real-time unity as well as the prospect of eternal life.

So what's the message?

Ephesians summarises the whole Christian message in 6 chapters. It begins with praise for a God who thought squitty little humans worth 'predestining' (which means actively drawing them back to himself). Then it tells us that we needed such drawing because we were dead to God. An infusion of spiritual life woke us up to him like Sleeping Beauty, the evil spell cast on us by the devil having been broken by Christ on the cross.

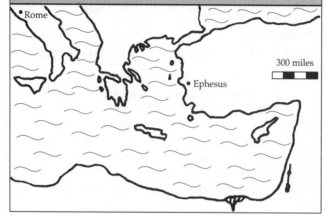

EPHESUS

Having received this 'new life' we then have the responsibility to live
it out. That includes maintaining the unity of the church, and allowing
God's Spirit to renew us inwardly so that we can have exemplary lives
outwardly. Husbands and wives (and everyone else) are told to submit to
each other out of love, and the devil gets a final bashing with the famous
passage about 'the armour of God' so that, having done all, we can still
stand faithful to the end. Try it.

Key verse

*In [Christ] we have redemption through his blood, the forgiveness of
sins, in accordance with the riches of God's grace that he lavished on us
with all wisdom and understanding.*

Ephesians 1:7,8

PAUL'S LETTER TO THE PHILIPPIANS

Overview
Written from prison, this could almost be Paul's last will and testament (except his letters to Timothy are later). It is certainly the one he would perhaps most wish to be remembered for by his closest friends. It is warm, personal, deep, spiritual and above all hopeful in the face of possible death.

He thanks the Philippians for a gift which eased the discomfort of his imprisonment. He says he doesn't mind if he lives, because that is more

---

TOP PERSONALITY – EPAPHRODITUS

Epaphroditus was one of Paul's companions. He was a native Philippian, sent as the church's messenger, and had obviously exceeded his responsibilities and ended up becoming ill, and he almost died from an unspecified illness, which sounds suspiciously like exhaustion brought on by over-work. A true saint, otherwise unknown.

---

useful work, or dies, because that is to be with Christ which is better still. Meanwhile, he intends to labour on because he's not perfect yet. And he pens a timeless hymn of praise about Christ.

Link to Christ
The hymn of chapter 2 is perhaps the most majestic poetry in the whole Bible, let alone in the New Testament (which doesn't have much poetry anyway). It celebrates Christ's coming as God in human form, his humility and his sacrifice, and rejoices in his eternal sovereignty.

So what's the message?
Billy Graham, the twentieth century evangelist, often said that he would never retire until God retired him (through death). He continued to preach even when partially disabled by Parkinson's Disease. That is something of Paul's thought here. There's no let up in the Christian life. There's always more to learn. There's always more to do. And above all, there's always more to change in one's own life and relationship with God.

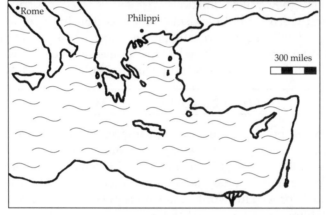

PHILIPPI

If that sounds like fanaticism, it is – in the nicest possible way. True sainthood, as both Paul and Epaphroditus demonstrated, means going the second mile (to borrow Jesus' phrase) and recognising that one is never quite up to God's standard of perfection. That's no cause for alarm; Paul knows he won't be rejected, because he has trusted in Christ. But he does feel responsible and grateful to God and won't rest on his laurels. It's a good example.

Key verse

At the name of Jesus every knee should bow, in heaven and on earth and under the earth, and every tongue confess that Jesus Christ is Lord, to the glory of God the Father.

Philippians 2:10,11

PAUL'S LETTER TO THE COLOSSIANS

Overview

'New Age' spirituality, which seems to embrace everything from crystals to zodiacs, is not new at all. The only surprising thing is why it's so popular in the new millennium.

You find it echoed in Colossians. Today its principles are wrapped in technological foil but underneath they're much the same as they ever were. No-one knows exactly what the Colossian 'heresy' was, but it included both Jewish elements and pagan mythology. Planetary worship

---

TOP PERSONALITY – MARK

John Mark puts in a surprise appearance. He was the cousin of Barnabas, Paul's first travelling companion, and probably the author of the Gospel of Mark. But he had fallen out of favour with Paul because he had deserted that first mission journey. Now he's obviously proved his worth, and Paul is pleased to commend him. One failure doesn't make a disaster.

---

was included. Paul treated it as a sceptic today would. Such things have no place in Christianity, even if they do demonstrate the universal spiritual hunger.

Link to Christ

Paul resorts to prose instead of the poetry of Philippians, but gives the Colossians an equally stirring and comprehensive statement about the supremacy of Jesus over everything in heaven and earth. Here is an explicit statement that Jesus is fully God, the creator and sustainer of all things.

So what's the message?

Well, having told the Romans, Galatians and Ephesians that Christ is all you need, Paul tells the Colossians that – guess what! – Christ is all you need. Only differently, not just because he was fed up with sounding like a scratched CD but because the Colossians had different needs. This time he's not so bothered about whether you get to heaven by faith or by effort, but about who Jesus really is in relation to everything and everyone else.

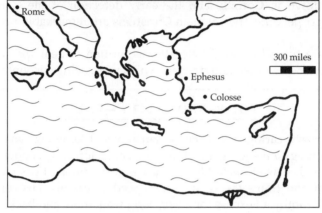

COLOSSE

The Colossians wanted 'freedom', a spiritual high that released them
from the daily drudge. They won't get it by adding 'New Age' stuff to
Christianity, he warns, but only by returning to simple faith in Christ.
Christ gives freedom from the bondage of sin (he forgives) and frees us
from bondage to rules and systems (he's superseded them) – but this is
still not freedom to do as you like. Rather, he sets us free to live as God
intended, in accordance with his laws, which is impossible without
Christ.

Key verse

> *God was pleased to have all his fullness dwell in him [Christ], and
> through him to reconcile to himself all things…by making peace
> through his blood, shed on the cross.*
>
> Colossians 1:19,20

113

PAUL'S FIRST LETTER TO THE THESSALONIANS

Overview

Thessalonica was a northern Greek city, a busy international port and one of the first big city churches planted by Paul. By contrast to the later troubles down in Corinth, and the early defection of the Galatians to 'another gospel', the Thessalonian Christians are remarkably normal and robust.

This is a typical pastoral letter. It was written to deal with questions which were being asked and dangers which were being encountered. And

---

TOP PERSONALITY – PAUL

Paul was a caring pastor. His anguish at not knowing what was happening to his fledgling church in Thessalonica was obviously intense. It wasn't helped by the fact that the phone lines weren't up yet and trains travelled at the speed of camels. His concern gave Timothy an excuse for a very long walk there and back.

---

there's some defensiveness about it too. It seems that jealous people were portraying Paul's brief visit as a failure, a hit and run mission. But if he hadn't run, he'd have been hit harder by rioters.

Link to Christ

Jesus spoke quite often to his undiscerning disciples about his promised return to earth. Paul had obviously heard about it from them, and had also discerned it for himself. This letter to the Thessalonians reinforces much of what Jesus said, and enhances the scanty New Testament teaching on the subject.

So what's the message?

In short, get ready and stay on your marks because you don't know when the gun will go off. When Paul wrote this he genuinely expected Jesus to return, and for the world to end during his own lifetime. Later he changed his view, and he looked forward to meeting Christ in heaven before the world ended.

Thessalonica

300 miles

Corinth

THESSALONICA

We just don't know when Jesus will return (or when we will die). While it's pretty unhealthy to go around morbidly assuming each day could be our last, there is some sense in remembering that life is short and uncertain. That way, you don't let yourself be drawn down life's blind alleys and you keep short accounts with God and with other people. Problems won't last forever. It's one of the Bible's recipes for emotional, as well as spiritual, health. It helps to reduce stress.

Key verse

So then, let us not be like others, who are asleep, but let us be alert and self-controlled.

1 Thessalonians 5:6

PAUL'S SECOND LETTER TO THE THESSALONIANS

Overview
This is a hastily-scribbled note dealing with issues which hadn't been fully clarified before. Once more, the end is nigh in Paul's thinking and he describes God as a fiery judge. (It could be that he's feeling pretty exasperated by the goings on in Corinth, where he is staying). Also, he is concerned about the end-of-the-world cult that is growing up north. Members of the cult are quitting their jobs, certain that Jesus is about to come back – they want to have a spiritual retreat first. Paul is saying that

---

TOP PERSONALITY – SILAS

Paul's co-writer and secretary was Silas, also known as Silvanus. He replaced Barnabas and Mark as Paul's travelling companion on his second mission journey, like Paul having the advantage of a Roman passport (it got them out of trouble). He was also well in with the Jews in Jerusalem who weren't always well-disposed to Paul. A useful guy to have around.

---

we must leave it to Christ to decide when the world will end and not look for signs (like comets in the night sky or the ending of the millennium) nor imagine he will swoop down to earth in a space-ship.

Link to Christ
With the continuing focus on Jesus' return, Paul introduces a fresh element: the man of lawlessness. Some form of satanic-inspired world ruler, it seems (there's been a few of those through history). But no matter who or what, says Paul, Jesus is ultimately stronger and the forces of evil cannot prevail against him for ever. Stirring stuff; pity it takes so long, though.

So what's the message?
If you were ever introduced to the now politically-incorrect stories of Noddy by Enid Blyton, you'll remember a kindly but authoritarian gentleman in blue uniform called PC (for police constable, not politically correct) Plod. And plod is what Paul advocates here. It's not very

TIME AND PLACE
Paul visited Thessalonica on his second and third
missionary journeys. He is writing from Corinth, about 6
months after he wrote his first letter to the Thessalonians
in AD 51/52. Thessalonica is modern-day Salonika
(which still boasts a first century arch). In Paul's day
Thessalonica was large and important, possibly housing
over 200,000 people.

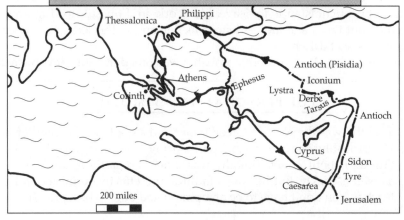

PAUL'S SECOND JOURNEY

glamorous, but like the PC it gets you where you need to be and gets the job done. Our problem is that we like to chase hares, never catch them and end up cross and unfulfilled.

Don't chase hare-brained ideas about the second coming, Paul says, and don't give up your day job in order to give more time to prayer. Just get on with living and believing the basic truths of Christianity. Plod. And why not? The pages of history are littered with the pathetic stories of people who thought they were wiser than God. There's more virtue in staying the course than in straying from it.

Key verse

*So then, brothers and sisters, stand firm and hold to the teachings we
passed on to you.*

2 Thessalonians 2:15

117

PAUL'S FIRST LETTER TO TIMOTHY

Overview
According to the autobiography of former British Prime Minister John Major, he suffered throughout his tenure of office from the 'back-seat driving' of his predecessor Margaret Thatcher. The apostle Paul had been forced by circumstance to leave his work in Ephesus to Timothy, a talented but timid and inexperienced leader, and in this letter Paul does a bit of back seat driving.

Unlike John Major, Timothy probably welcomed it. Paul's involvement

---

TOP PERSONALITY – TIMOTHY

Timothy was the son of a Greek father and a godly Jewish mother. He probably became a Christian during Paul's visit to Lystra (Turkey) about AD 49. Timothy was quiet and easily intimidated, as well as sickly. But he was a faithful and effective minister and teacher. You don't have to be an opinionated bore to be a preacher.

---

added to Timothy's authority, which was apparently being questioned. The letter reveals how first century local churches were organised. It also provides timeless principles of Christian leadership – especially for dealing with opposition from within the church.

Link to Christ
Paul starts the letter by referring to his own testimony of faith, saying that there's hope for anyone if he, 'the worst of sinners' could be saved by Jesus. He uses this letter to remind Timothy that the ministry of Jesus was primarily to 'save sinners' from life and death without God.

So what's the message?
Much of the letter deals with the character of church leaders and matters of church organisation. Two things emerge. One is that anyone carrying responsibility within the church (including practical tasks like planning the rotas as well as the allegedly more 'spiritual' roles of teaching and counselling) should be of sound faith and morals before being 'ordained'.

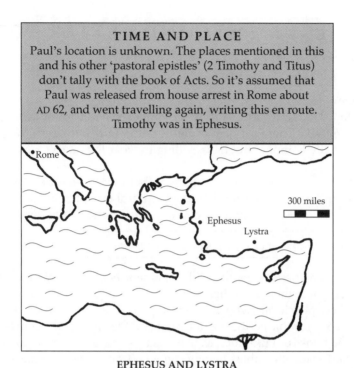

EPHESUS AND LYSTRA

The second is that relationships within the church are to be disciplined. Try telling people today what to do and you could end up with your face plastered all over the tabloid press, but in Paul's day Christians recognised that if some were called to lead, the others were responsible to accept that leadership. Those were the days.

Key verse

Fight the good fight of the faith. Take hold of the eternal life to which you were called.

1 Timothy 6:12

PAUL'S SECOND LETTER TO TIMOTHY

Overview

This, almost certainly, is the last letter Paul ever wrote (or at least, the last one preserved). There's a note of desperation in it as he sees the painful end of his life looming. But he is willing to wear the martyr's crown with pride.

So there's less about church life than there was in the first letter. Paul focuses on the eternal rather than the temporal except to bemoan the fact that he's made a lot of enemies and even his friends have deserted him.

TOP PERSONALITY – LUKE

There is a friend, says the Old Testament book of Proverbs, who sticks closer than a brother or sister. Such a person is Luke, 'the beloved physician' who had accompanied Paul on some of his journeys, chronicled the life of Christ and the story of the church in (in the books of Luke and Acts) and is now the only companion left at Paul's side, the others having signed off sick or gone home early.

He reminds Timothy to stand up for the gospel. It's sober reading, but we need reminding that life isn't a bed of roses.

Link to Christ

Paul is about to find out about the truth of death at first hand – no longer as a matter of theory or debate. And Paul clings to the fundamental apostolic belief: that Jesus is raised from the dead. That is the source of all hope for the eternal future.

So what's the message?

The word 'shame' turns up rather often in this letter. Paul is not ashamed of being in prison, and he serves God with a clear conscience. He says that Onesiphorus (whoever he was) unlike most others wasn't ashamed to visit him in jail (presumably risking arrest as a sympathiser in the process). And he urges Timothy to be ashamed neither of the helpless Paul nor the gospel he has preached.

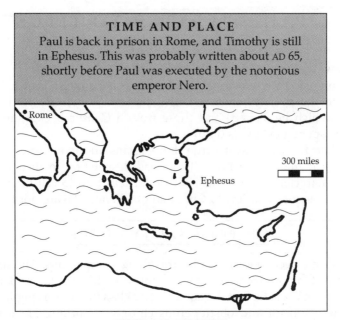

ROME AND EPHESUS

When you look back on your life, there are usually some things you're ashamed of, and some things you're pleased with. To be able to say, with Paul, 'I'm not ashamed of what I've done nor of who I've served' is something special. Today, people are willing to talk about spirituality, but many are still shy about being identified as disciples of Christ.

Key verse

Here is a trustworthy saying: If we died with him, we will also live with him; if we endure, we will also reign with him.

2 Timothy 2:11,12

PAUL'S LETTER TO TITUS

Overview

Before you read this, remember that Paul was not a racist. He tried to heal the rift in the church between Christians from a strongly Jewish background (which he shared) and those from a Gentile background (with whom he spent most of his time).

So when he says that it's true that Cretans are liars, brutes and lazy gluttons – it must have been. Titus was despatched to deal with this national characteristic and this short letter tells him to call the islanders (renowned as mercenaries) to Christian obedience. We are not told if his

---

TOP PERSONALITY – TITUS

Titus had been one of Paul's travelling companions. He spent much of his ministry as Paul's deputy in tricky places. Before serving in Crete he had the equally thankless task of serving in the equally difficult and obstreperous church at Corinth. He was a Gentile, and someone once suggested he was Luke's brother.

---

mission was a success. It would have been a miracle if it was, but some jobs just have to be done, anyway.

Link to Christ

Jesus once said that 'if you love me, you will keep my commandments'. That seems to be in Paul's mind in this letter as he stresses that the Cretans need to match their professed Christian faith with some simple Christian behaviour, instead of continuing to loaf around like lager louts on holiday.

So what's the message?

Titus is a rag-bag of instructions (similar to those given in 1 Timothy) about the character and responsibilities of church leaders. Unlike the Cretans, leaders are not to be hot-blooded, violent and greedy. Titus had to do the job himself, the locals being singularly disqualified.

However, he would have to 'grow' leaders locally or else the church would die, and Titus provides an indirect reminder that people who become Christians undergo an inner change of heart. Living the Christian life involves obedience to God, as Paul advocates, but such obedience is

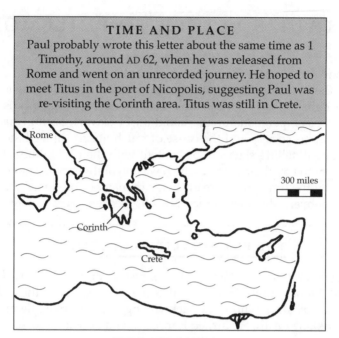

CRETE AND CORINTH

only fully possible when a person receives the spiritual desire to obey
God rather than their own drives. The letter, in fact, is saying no more
than 'live like Jesus'. If the Cretans could be expected to do it, anyone can.

Key verse

*Remind the people to be subject to rulers and authorities, to be
obedient, to be ready to do whatever is good, to slander no-one, to be
peaceable and considerate, and to show true humility towards
everyone.*

Titus 3:1,2

PAUL'S LETTER TO PHILEMON

Overview

One of those unanswerable theological questions that students have a habit of debating over undrinkable coffee at unearthly hours is why St Paul never campaigned for the abolition of slavery, seeing that it was endemic in his society and the cause of much misery. Indeed, he seemed to condone it, telling slaves to be content with their lot (although he did tell masters to pay their wages, which was revolutionary in some places).

Well, by the time you've read this, you may be convinced that he did at least subvert the institution. He has befriended a runaway slave

---

TOP PERSONALITY – ONESIMUS

Onesimus is no Spartacus but he's just as brave. He must have had a lot of faith in Paul (as well as in God) because in those days a runaway slave who went back willingly to his erstwhile master was risking death. He turned himself in and hoped for leniency.

(Onesimus) who 'belongs' to another friend, Philemon. Paul obeys the law (sending the runaway home) and at the same time asks for his release. Clever. And that's not all…

Link to Christ

Paul wants Philemon to set his slave Onesimus free (so he can go back and continue to help Paul) but Paul sends him back and leaves the decision to Philemon. All parties to this strange deal were banking on each other to honour Christ. It provides a good example of what Jesus meant by self-giving 'fellowship' within the church.

So what's the message?

Paul's letter to Philemon raises the question: 'What should Christians do about endemic social evils?' It's not fair to say (as some do) that Paul largely ignored slavery. In 1 Timothy he said that slave trading was 'contrary to sound doctrine'. He outlawed trade in humans by Christians, and urged fair treatment all round.

COLOSSE AND ROME

To have joined the political activists campaigning for abolition (and there were some in the Roman empire) would have been to ally the young church with a radical minority which would have discredited its total message. The church needed to become well-established first. Christianity isn't about abolishing slavery, it's about discovering the spiritual freedom of knowing Christ, and then applying that in daily life. And that's exactly what Paul invites Onesimus and Philemon to do. Meanwhile, note that Paul does the right thing (sending the slave home) *and* finds a way of ensuring that the slave survives. That's 'wisdom'.

Key verse

He is very dear to me but even dearer to you, both as a person and as a fellow believer in the Lord.

Philemon 16

THE LETTER TO THE HEBREWS

Overview

Avoid the book of Hebrews until you've dipped into the Old Testament and also got the hang of Paul's letters to the Romans and the Galatians. This letter was written for Jews steeped in the practices of temple-based Judaism, last heard of in AD 70.

Once you are aware of that background, however, you'll see what a superb parallel can be drawn between the Old Testament and the life, death and resurrection of Christ. Hebrews sets out to answer the doubts of some Christians who weren't sure how to relate their old and new lives.

If you still want to dip into Hebrews begin with chapter 11, which is

---

TOP PERSONALITY – MELCHIZADEK

Let's have a tongue-twister as 'top personality'. Just when you thought you'd left the Old Testament priesthood 600 pages ago, Melchizadek is saluted here as an ideal priest. He is regarded as a 'type' (picture) of Christ because in the biblical record he has no recorded parentage or death and hence appears to be 'eternal'. Abraham gave him tithes, which made Melchizadek greater than Abraham himself – as was Jesus.

---

for anyone. It's all about faith, and it gives a good mini-history of the Old Testament story.

Link to Christ

The purpose of this letter to the Hebrews is to demonstrate the superiority of Christ over all that had gone before (Abraham, Moses, even the angels in heaven). Christ fulfilled the Old Testament symbolism of sacrifice. He is the High Priest par excellence, who has taken a sacrifice for sin (himself) into the Holy of Holies (heaven) thus opening up the way for us to follow.

So what's the message?

The message is simple: Jesus is the greatest thing since Adam sliced the apple. Everything the Jews sought in terms of spiritual rapprochement with God through their elaborate customs has been fulfilled in Christ. He is therefore the true Messiah, the Son of God who has now rendered the old system obsolete.

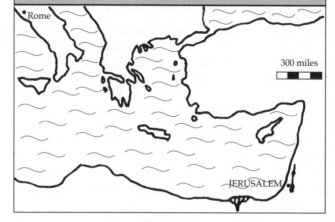

JERUSALEM

Hebrews also contains the Bible's sternest warnings about the risk of falling away from God (and not being able to get back on board), and some of its clearest statements about the divinity of Christ. The famous passage on faith in chapter 11, is about having confidence in what is unseen.

Key verse

Now faith is being sure of what we hope for and certain of what we do not see.

Hebrews 11:1

THE LETTER OF JAMES

Overview

This is a letter for men of action. It's robust, hard-hitting, no-nonsense practical stuff. James wants none of this mystical, syrupy, lovey-dovey romanticism that oozes out of some 'devotional' books, sermons and songs. He wants action.

Strangely, Martin Luther (who was also a man of action) reckoned this was 'an epistle of straw' and said it should never have been in the Bible. But he believed (wrongly) that it contradicted Paul – which it doesn't. (Incidentally, Luther was an amazing man who nailed his own theses to

---

TOP PERSONALITY – JAMES

The author is probably James, the brother of Jesus. (The other James, the apostle and brother of John, was killed in AD 44). So he's also a carpenter's son, who opposed his brother Jesus for a while, before having a private resurrection appearance (according to Paul) and never looking back.

He led the church in Jerusalem and appeared as its spokesman during the first church council held in the city (recorded in Acts 15).

---

the church door, and was so conscious of the devil that he once threw an inkpot at him! It sailed across his monk's cell and hit the wall – and the stain is still there).

Link to Christ

Apart from the family link (James was Christ's brother) there's a good few echoes of the Sermon on the Mount here. James knows, perhaps better than most, that Jesus was a stern critic of hypocrisy: i.e. saying you have faith but not applying it.

So what's the message?

If you want to be religious, get off your butt and get out into the world and do some good with your time, your tongue, your talent and your chequebook. Luther's concern was that this stark message contradicted Paul's teaching about being saved by faith alone (James actually says that faith without works is useless). But James isn't saying you can work your

JERUSALEM

way into God's good books. He says that once in God's good books (through faith in Christ) *then* you've got to show it. If your life contradicts your profession of faith, you may be deluding yourself.

James has some stern words for the rich (pay up) and for those who fawn to them (don't, because they're as sinful as the poor, if not more so). He also says: if you've nothing good to say, keep your mouth shut, be kind, pray hard, and let God fill your diary. Who said Christianity was a soft option?

Key verse

Faith, by itself, if it is not accompanied by action, is dead.

James 2:17

THE FIRST LETTER OF PETER

Overview
Life is full of surprises. This letter, written by the blundering big-mouthed fisherman turns out to be gentle and pastorally sensitive. And despite the fact that Peter was once rebuked by Paul for not mixing with Gentiles (which was hypocritical of Peter since he had been the first to preach that Jews and Gentiles were equal – having had an important dream telling him so) there's plenty here that echoes the teaching of Paul. It is amazing that Peter and Paul, so totally different in personality, were able to share the message without splitting into 2 factions.

TOP PERSONALITY – PETER

We've had Peter before (and also his collaborators Mark and Silas) but he bears another mention as he approaches the end of his colourful life. Age has not wearied him, but it has mellowed him. He advocates self-control and humility – neither of which had been strengths in his youth!

This letter is meant to encourage people who are finding life tough. It is an uncompromising spur to hold on to faith and maintain a consistent public witness.

Link to Christ
This is a very Christ-centred letter, with a simple and clear statement that 'Christ died for our sins'. But only Peter adds that Jesus' suffering is (amongst other things) an example to follow. Jesus did not retaliate when unjustly punished, but instead trusted his heavenly Father to sort the rats out.

So what's the message?
The great thing about the way the Bible is arranged is that there's a lot of fresh stuff as you get near the end – it doesn't get tired and start repeating itself like a forgetful lecturer. Peter introduces a couple of concepts which we've heard before, but in a fresh way. We are to be holy, as God is holy. That was the Old Testament message, but Peter spells it out. God is our role model and the standard by which all our words and deeds are to be measured.

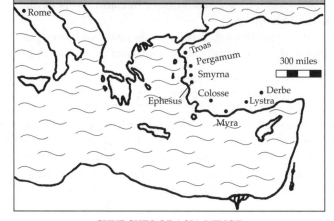

Rome

Troas

Pergamum

Smyrna

300 miles

Colosse

Derbe

Ephesus

Lystra

Myra

CHURCHES OF ASIA MINOR

But don't be disheartened. Peter also tells us that those who have
trusted Christ are a 'royal priesthood and a chosen people'. This is where
the teaching about 'the priesthood of all believers' comes from. We have
direct access to God. Ministers are a good thing, says Peter, but they are
not mediators between us and God. They are servants to help and
encourage us.

Key verse

*You are a chosen people, a royal priesthood, a holy nation, a people
belonging to God, that you may declare the praises of him who called
you out of darkness into his wonderful light.*

1 Peter 2:9

THE SECOND LETTER OF PETER

Overview
This letter is a brilliant flowing piece of invective against false teachers, calling them all the names under the sun and reserving for them for the pits of God's judgement. Written before the days of libel laws, this letter, if delivered as a speech today, would have to claim parliamentary privilege in order to avoid a lawsuit.

Wonderfully entertaining, this letter also packs a heavy punch. It starts and finishes with a warning: 'Make sure you're on the right side.' And

---

TOP PERSONALITY – 'ANON'

Let's be different and make 'Anon' our top personality (since no-one is certain who wrote this letter). There are a lot of Anons in the Bible. They get everywhere. And there are a lot of Anons in the world today, too. They *are* everywhere, often identified only by their social security numbers. But God knows their names – and ours.

---

even if you are, make sure you don't get seduced away from it by some plausible new ideas. Or else you'll fall into the pit, too. Gulp.

Link to Christ
The author of this letter has been told, by Christ, that he's about to die. Not the sort of information most of us want to hear. But it certainly concentrates the author's mind wonderfully. He can get ready. We too can get ready, even though we don't know the exact date of our death.

So what's the message?
The author focuses on revelation – God's various communications to humankind. The prophets of old spoke as they were moved by the Holy Spirit (rather like yachts being blown along by the wind). But the false teachers of his own day are not speaking by the Holy Spirit; they've made up colourful stories and extravagant claims.

Their teaching doesn't conform to what has been handed down by the apostles. And so the writer of this letter gives us a tool with which to

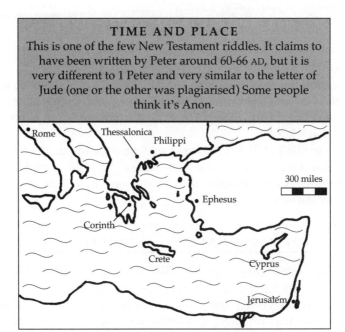

TIME AND PLACE
This is one of the few New Testament riddles. It claims to have been written by Peter around 60-66 AD, but it is very different to 1 Peter and very similar to the letter of Jude (one or the other was plagiarised) Some people think it's Anon.

Rome
Thessalonica
Philippi
300 miles
Ephesus
Corinth
Crete
Cyprus
Jerusalem

THE NEW TESTAMENT WORLD

handle the claims and counter-claims that have bombarded ordinary Christians ever since. Check back on what Jesus, Paul and the others actually said, before you accept what Bishop Freshman or Brother Bombast are reported as saying. Being a Bishop or a Brother offers no immunity from divine prosecution.

Key verse

If you do these things, you will never fall, and you will receive a rich welcome into the eternal kingdom of our Lord and Saviour Jesus Christ.

2 Peter 1:10,11

THE 3 LETTERS OF JOHN

Overview

We're lumping the two tiny second and third letters of John with the more substantial first letter, because they don't say anything that can't be put in a single sentence. (And when you cut out the personal gush in both, that's about all that's left.)

Here is gentle but firm devotional writing, focusing on the love of God and commending the practice of love in everyday life. Firmly based on the premise that Christ lovingly died for our sins, John is urging us to love sacrificially ourselves.

TOP PERSONALITY – A CHOSEN LADY

Women don't feature much in our list of 'top personalities' but John's second letter is addressed to an anonymous 'chosen lady'. Some have suggested 'she' is a church but that's taking things a bit far. She was probably a wealthy woman who hosted church meetings (presumably while her husband was down the pub).

Link to Christ

John is especially anxious to stress the humanity of Christ, because some heretics were saying that 'Christ' only *seemed* to be a man. John reminds his readers that he actually saw, heard and touched the great teacher and saviour. After all, the author had been 'the beloved disciple' slumped against Jesus at the Last Supper, and you couldn't get much closer to the Lord than that.

So what's the message?

John holds that fine and difficult balance between correct teaching and applied faith. He wants everyone to be certain that Jesus Christ really was God incarnate; fully divine and fully human in an inexplicable but unmistakable mix. The life and death of Jesus was a huge sacrifice of love in order to deal with the problem of sin separating people from God.

He stresses that Christ's love is an example to be followed by all. He gives practical examples of love in action: no favouritism in the church, no hatred, offering hospitality to genuine missionaries. Yet false teachers are

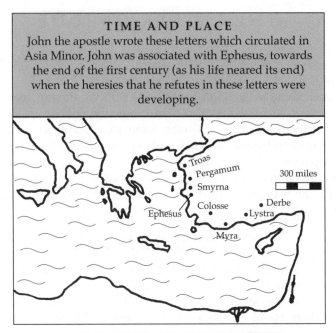

SOME OF THE CHURCHES OF ASIA MINOR

not to be tolerated and those who claim to be teachers are to be tested
before their words are accepted.

John's first letter also contains a much-needed note of assurance. How
do I know that at the end of the day (and especially the end of the world)
God really will accept me? Just ask yourself one question, John says. Do
you trust Christ as the way to God or not? If so, you're OK. If not – why
not? You've got nothing to lose, except a God of love.

Key verse

God has given us eternal life, and this life is in his Son. Those who have
the Son have life; those who do not have the Son of God do not have life.
1 John 5:11,12

THE LETTER OF JUDE

Overview
If this letter sounds familiar, it's because you've already read 2 Peter. Virtually every verse here is also there. Someone cribbed from someone else, but scholars are not sure who went first. So once more, we are reminded to stand firm on the faith and beware false teachers for whom is reserved doom and gloom

Interestingly, this isn't the letter the author intended to write. Apparently he was going to write a treatise about becoming and being a

---

TOP PERSONALITY – JUDE

The author calls himself the brother of James and is almost certainly the Jude who is listed among the brothers (or half-brothers) of Jesus. James became very well known, but Jude was obviously a kid brother. He obviously came to believe in Christ, too, but we don't know how or when.

Christian. Unfortunately, if he ever got round to writing the intended letter no one thought to preserve a copy for us.

Link to Christ
Jude calls himself a 'servant' of Jesus. He is fond of calling Jesus 'Lord' and that reminds us of Christ's risen and ascended sovereignty. This gives Jude the perfect right to criticize these slimy slanderers and false teachers who confuse the flock of God – which he does with passion.

So what's the message?
When people teach things that oppose the apostles' basic principles, they ought to be spoken against. Mercy, peace and love (which Jude sends to his readers) does not exclude standing up for what is right.

The famous words at the end of Jude shine like the sun through a hole in a storm cloud. It is both a prayer and a reassuring statement. Trust God and he will keep you safe through all the changing scenes of life, because he alone has all power and authority in heaven and on earth. Once again, Jude hits that New Testament balance. Just prior to this reassurance he has

THE ROMAN EMPIRE

told his readers to keep themselves in God's love. Being a Christian is a relationship of willing dependence on a powerful God.

Key verse

To the only God our Saviour be glory, majesty, power and authority, through Jesus Christ our Lord, before all ages, now and for evermore! Amen.

Jude 25

REVELATION

Overview
This is the last book of the Bible but it's not exactly the sports report. It is full of colourful symbolism which is hard to equate with anything known to man, beast or historian.

Revelation is not a count-down to the End of the World (as some people think) but a series of visions of the world as it is. Surreal, Salvador Dali-like pictures of the world in all its mess and evil. And, hovering over it all, a sovereign God who's shining his torch into the darkness and moving history towards completion.

TOP PERSONALITY – JOHN

It was written by John the apostle. Despite his location, on the Greek island of Patmos, he's not on holiday but in a prison camp for his faith. He's old, in his nineties, and he's outlived most if not all of those who saw Jesus alive. And he's kept the faith. Wonderful.

Link to Christ
John claimed he had had a direct vision from God, and Revelation depicts Jesus sitting on the throne of heaven in both judgement and mercy. The poetic description of him in chapter 1 has given rise to the unfortunate image of God with long white hair sitting on a cloud, old and 'past it'. But there's nothing 'past it' about this Christ; he's on fire with passion and energy.

So what's the message?
Put yourself into the shoes of first century Christians facing the ire (and fire) of Roman officials who reckoned that a monotheistic religion that wasn't Judaism (which had special government dispensation) was blasphemy (because it denied any other gods, including the emperor). So as the bullyboys torch your home or string you up, where's this great God of yours? And when will Jesus keep his promise to come back and rescue you?

This series of visions (the book can be divided and subdivided into blocks of 7) suggests that evil has always rampaged, and always will.

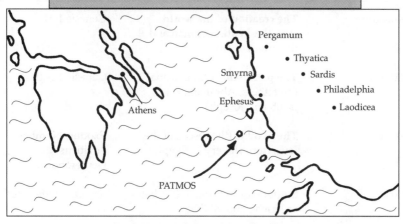

THE 7 CHURCHES OF REVELATION

However, God is still supreme. He supports his people and promises
them eternity with him, if they remain faithful to him. One day evil will
be eliminated by the return of Christ. Which was good news then, and
continues to be good news now.

Key verse

*He will wipe away every tear from their eyes. There will be no more
death or mourning or crying or pain, for the old order of things has
passed away.*

Revelation 21:4

THE BIBLE STORY AT A GLANCE

DATES (approximately)	PERIOD	BIBLE BOOKS
Prehistory	**The creation of the world** (and the creation of man and the origin of sin)	Genesis 1-11
2000 BC	**The patriarchs** (Our spiritual forefathers, Abraham, Isaac, Jacob and Joseph)	Genesis 12-50
1300 BC	**The Exodus** (the rescue of the Jews from slavery in Egypt)	Exodus, Numbers Leviticus, Deuteronomy
1200 BC	**Settlement in Canaan** (the battle of Jericho and all that)	Joshua, Judges, Ruth
1000 BC	**The first kings** Saul, David and Solomon (who reigned for about 40 years each)	1 and 2 Samuel, 1 Kings, 1 Chronicles Psalms (those by David) Proverbs, Ecclesiastes, Song of Songs
900 BC	**The divided kingdom** (Israel in the north, and Judah in the south. Israel only lasted 200 years)	1 and 2 Kings 2 Chronicles Amos (N), Hosea (N) Isaiah (S), Micah (S), Jonah, Joel
722 BC	**Israel is destroyed** But Judah lasts another 140 years	2 Kings, 2 Chronicles, Isaiah, Jeremiah, Lamentations, Nahum, Habakkuk, Zephaniah

DATES (approximately)	PERIOD	BIBLE BOOKS
587 BC	**Judah is destroyed and exiled to Babylon** (The exile lasted about 50 years)	Jeremiah, Ezekiel, Daniel, Obadiah
537 BC	**The Restoration** (The Jews returned to their homeland over the next 100 years)	Ezra, Nehemiah, Esther, Haggai, Zechariah, Malachi
440 BC – 0 BC	**THE INTER-TESTAMENTAL PERIOD** (400 years under the Greeks and Romans)	No Bible books cover this period
0-33 AD	**Life of Christ**	Matthew, Mark, Luke, John
33-60 AD	**The early church**	Acts of the Apostles
49-65 AD	**The early church**	Letters by Paul, John, James and others
90 AD	**The whole story of the church**	Revelation

The Books of the Old Testament

GENESIS · EXODUS · LEVITICUS · NUMBERS · DEUTERONOMY

THE LAW

JOSHUA · JUDGES · RUTH · 1 & 2 SAMUEL · 1 & 2 KINGS · 1 & 2 CHRONICLES · EZRA · NEHEMIAH · ESTHER

HISTORY

JOB · PSALMS · PROVERBS · ECCLESIASTES · SONG OF SOLOMON · LAMENTATIONS

POETRY AND WISDOM

ISAIAH · JEREMIAH · EZEKIEL · DANIEL

MAJOR PROPHETS

HOSEA · JOEL · AMOS · OBADIAH · JONAH · MICAH · NAHUM · HABAKKUK · ZEPHANIAH · HAGGAI · ZECHARIAH · MALACHI

MINOR PROPHETS

A SUMMARY OF EACH BOOK

Old Testament Books

The books of 'law'

Genesis 1–11	The prologue – about the beginning of the universe, the beginning of man and the beginning of sin.
Genesis 12–50	Abraham's family – God starts with an odd bunch
Exodus	Moses rescues his people from slavery
Leviticus	Ancient rules for hygiene and holiness
Numbers	Lost in the desert
Deuteronomy	Moses' final speeches show God in a good light

History books

Joshua	Conquering the promised land
Judges	Cycles of sin (and the brake of God)
Ruth	A Moabite woman finds God and a husband
1 Samuel	Israel chooses Saul – a manic depressive – as king
2 Samuel	King David, a man after God's own heart
1 Kings	King Solomon the great
2 Kings	The 2 kingdoms and how they fell.
1, 2 Chronicles	The story of Kings retold from a religious perspective
Ezra	Re-building the temple (after the exile)
Nehemiah	Re-building the walls of Jerusalem
Esther	A beautiful heroine rescues her people from genocide

Wisdom books

Job	Why do bad things happen to good people?
Psalms	The Hebrew hymn book (plus real emotions)
Proverbs	A collection of wise sayings (like 'a stitch in time', only wiser)
Ecclesiastes	The Emptiness of life without God
Song of Solomon	Love and sex, as invented by God

Major prophets

Isaiah	Soaring visions of God's greatness
Jeremiah	The sad and reluctant prophet
Lamentations	Poem about the misery of exile
Ezekiel	Zany visions and messages from God
Daniel	Colourful stories of faith in adversity

12 Minor prophets

Hosea	An unfaithful wife bares the truth
Joel	A plague of locusts warns of worse to come
Amos	Don't trample on the needy
Obadiah	Doom for the Edomites (serves them right)
Jonah	A fishy tale of human folly
Micah	Act justly, love mercy, walk humbly (simple but tricky)
Nahum	The destruction of Nineveh is foretold
Habakkuk	The Babylonians are even worse than the Assyrians
Zephaniah	Judah will be judged
Haggai	Re-build the temple!
Zechariah	Re-build the temple – the Messiah is coming!
Malachi	God will judge us

The Books of the New Testament

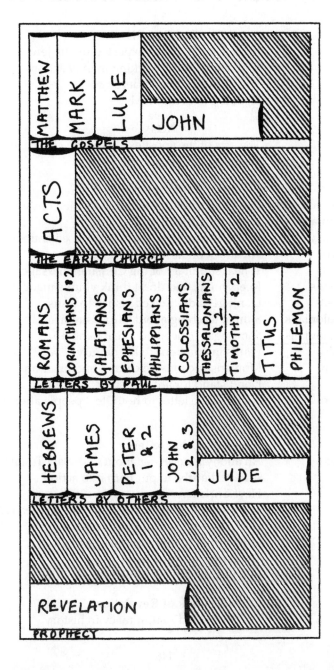

New Testament Books

The Gospels

Matthew	Jesus is the Messiah expected by the Jews
Mark	Jesus the miracle-working man of action
Luke	Jesus cares for the underdogs
John	Jesus is the Great I AM

Acts

Acts	The acts of the apostles – the early church grows and expands

Paul's letters

Romans	Paul's doctoral thesis on God's plan of salvation
1 Corinthians	If you are Christian, live like it
2 Corinthians	Paul's encouragement to a confused church
Galatians	An attack on false teaching
Ephesians	A neat summary of the Christian message
Philippians	Keep going, and don't think you've made it
Colossians	Don't get side-tracked – stick to Jesus
1 Thessalonians	Simple teaching about Christ's return
2 Thessalonians	Same again (they had a real hang up)
1 Timothy	Paul's instructions to his deputy
2 Timothy	More instructions on church organization
Titus	Don't stand for any nonsense in Crete
Philemon	An unsubtle letter to re-unite 2 people after an argument

Other letters

Hebrews	An anonymous essay about Old-New Testament links
James	A fiery diatribe to put faith into action
1 Peter	Hey! Christians are special to God
2 Peter	The day of the Lord is coming (are you ready?)
1 John	God's love is great; how is yours?
2 John	Look out lady, don't let people fool you
3 John	Stand firm on your faith
Jude	Evil people will get punished

The Book of Revelation

Revelation	Visions of God's supremacy in history

THE TEN COMMANDMENTS

- You shall have no other gods before me.

- You shall not worship false idols.

- You shall not take the name of the Lord in vain.

- You shall keep the Sabbath day holy.

- Honour your father and your mother.

- You shall not murder.

- You shall not commit adultery.

- You shall not steal.

- You shall not give false witness against your neighbour.

- You shall not covet your neighbour's house, or your neighbour's wife, or anything that belongs to your neighbour.

The ten commandments are described in the book of Exodus chapter 20. The commandments were designed to lead the Israelites to a life of practical holiness. Notice that the first 4 concern our attitude to God. The Israelites had just come from Egypt, a land of many idols. Today we still have many idols: money, fame, work, computers, gadgets, television and possessions. We may not intend to worship these things but if we spend time thinking about them and relying on them for our sense of identity then they have become 'gods' which prevent God from being central to our lives. Notice that the Sabbath – taking a day off a week to rest from our work and focus on God – is one of the ten commandments, given equal importance to not murdering. Not resting for at least one full day a week is a sin, and will therefore lead us into all sorts of difficulties. To covet means to desire something with evil motivation. To break God's commandments inwardly is just as bad as breaking them outwardly.

ANNUAL JEWISH FESTIVALS

FESTIVAL	JEWISH NAME	COMMENTS
*Passover	Pesach	This festival, that occurs at the beginning of the agricultural year, celebrates rescue from slavery in Egypt. The Passover meal has symbolic elements of roasted lamb, unleavened bread (they fled before there was time for it to rise) bitter herbs and 4 cups of wine at specific points, and ends with the words 'Next year in Jerusalem'.
*Pentecost (Or the Feast of Weeks, or First Fruits)	Shavuot	This festival celebrates the end of the 7 weeks of Barley harvest, and also became recognized as the anniversary of the giving of the Law at Sinai. It became important to Christians because it was the day the Holy Spirit descended on the disciples after Christ's death.
*Feast of Tabernacles (or Booths)	Sukkot	A week long festival at the end of the agricultural year, when all Israelites must live in shelters (booths) made of palm leaves to celebrate God's provision for them in the wilderness. A ceremony of water pouring recognizes the gift of rain from God.
Day of Atonement	Yom Kippur	The most solemn day of the year, now enshrined in complex religious rules, but originally the day the high priest confessed the sins of the people over the head of a goat then released it into the wilderness, to carry away their sins (the origin of the word 'scapegoat').

* The 3 main festivals are Pilgrim Festivals, when everyone tried to travel to Jerusalem, the central place of worship, as decreed by Moses in Deuteronomy. They were also agricultural festivals, as well as commemorations of God's freeing them from slavery, giving them the Law, and preserving them in the wilderness.

FESTIVAL	JEWISH NAME	COMMENTS
Purim	Purim	Celebrates the survival of the Jewish people in Persia in 470 BC. The evil Haman was defeated by the courage of Esther. Traditionally the book of Esther is read, and the congregation shouts and boos whenever the name of Haman is mentioned.

The festivals given above are the biblical festivals – other traditional Jewish festivals also occur.

Hanukkah (The Festival of Lights) is not mentioned in the Bible. It is one of the traditional Jewish festivals, and celebrates the survival of the Jewish Faith in 164 BC, when the Seleucids tried to destroy the Jewish religion, and when they wanted to re-dedicate the temple in Jerusalem to Zeus. Candles are burned for 8 days, because the sacred oil ran out, but miraculously burned for 8 days. (See the time-line of the temple in Jerusalem, in 2 Chronicles on page 37).

APPENDIX 5

THE GREAT EMPIRES THAT AFFECTED THE ISRAELITES

| 721 BC | **THE ASSYRIAN EMPIRE** |

721 BC — **THE ASSYRIAN EMPIRE**
The Assyrians destroyed the Northern kingdom of Israel and scattered the people so they could never return.

612 BC — **THE BABYLONIAN EMPIRE**
The Babylonians conquered the Assyrians and then took the people of Judah into exile in Babylon.

539 BC — **THE PERSIAN EMPIRE**
The Persian Empire conquered the Babylonian Empire, and allowed the exiles to go home to Jerusalem.

331 BC — **THE GREEK EMPIRE**
Alexander the Great defeated the Persians. The Greeks were the ruling empire for most of the inter-testamental period.

63 BC — **THE ROMAN EMPIRE**
Judea became a province of the Roman Empire.

THE HISTORY OF THE BIBLE

The Bible is a collection of 66 books (the word 'Bible' comes from the word 'biblia' meaning books) written by numerous authors over about 1500 years. Its unity of message is all the more remarkable for that. Few people could read or write in Old Testament times, and most people would have heard the stories and laws by word of mouth. But they were also written down from an early stage and edited from time to time throughout the period. Hundreds of manuscripts have been found, all copied from older manuscripts (and occasionally mistakes were made).

The Old Testament (39 books) was written in Hebrew. There were other languages around, but Hebrew was the language of Jewish worship. Most of the books of the Old Testament were probably agreed to be 'God's word' around 400 BC. *A Greek translation* of the Old Testament was made in 200 BC (known as the 'Septuagint' because it was written by 70 scholars) which was the version that Jesus and St Paul used.

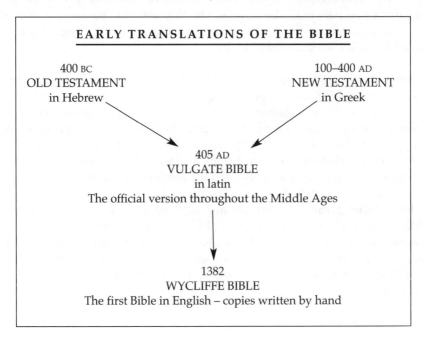

EARLY TRANSLATIONS OF THE BIBLE

400 BC
OLD TESTAMENT
in Hebrew

100–400 AD
NEW TESTAMENT
in Greek

405 AD
VULGATE BIBLE
in latin
The official version throughout the Middle Ages

1382
WYCLIFFE BIBLE
The first Bible in English – copies written by hand

The New Testament (27 books) was written in Greek, the 'English' – the universal language – of the first century. (Latin was only the 'official' language of the Roman Empire, used for legal documents). Books were finally chosen to be included in the NT if they were written by the apostles or those close to them. The final collection of New Testament books – the 'canon' – was not *finally* agreed until 400 AD, and one or two books were disputed for a while longer.

Early Bible manuscripts had to be copied by hand on scrolls made of papyrus (stems of the papyrus plant) or parchment, but by 200 AD the manuscripts were usually in the form of a 'codex' (sheets of parchment stitched together to form a book). Hundreds of early manuscripts of both testaments have been discovered, and by comparing them scholars have been able to agree a definitive and reliable text. The ancient manuscripts were written without punctuation. The Bible was only divided into chapters in the early 1200s by Stephen Langton.

A Latin translation of the whole Bible was made in 400 AD (Latin having superceded Greek as the universal language, much to the regret of later generations of schoolchildren). This was the Vulgate Bible (from 'vulgar' meaning popular) made by Jerome. The Vulgate Bible became the official version throughout the Middle Ages, but it meant the Bible was only available to those educated in Latin.

The Hebrew Old Testament became difficult to read (once Hebrew ceased to be a spoken language) so the Massorites (a group of Jewish scholars) put the vowels back in (to indicate the correct pronounciation) which the early Hebrews had omitted (because it's a very slow job copying millions of letters in fine pen strokes). This took them 400 years! This Massoretic text was finished in 916 AD, and became the standard Hebrew Bible (our OT), all later versions being copies of it.

The famous Dead Sea Scrolls are 1000 years older than the oldest Massoretic text and yet remarkably similar – proof of the reliability of the Jewish scribes who copied the Hebrew text down the centuries. The scrolls were found in 1948 by a shepherd in caves near Qumran (north of the Dead sea). Scholars have argued ever since over ownership of the 500 documents.

EARLY ENGLISH BIBLES

1526
TYNDALE NEW TESTAMENT
Based on the original manuscripts

↓

1535
COVERDALE BIBLE
first *full* Bible in English

↓

1611
AUTHORISED (KING JAMES) VERSION
Translated by a committee and the most important version for the
next 300 years

↓

1881
REVISED VERSION

John Wycliffe made an English translation of the Vulgate in 1382. He was persecuted for doing it, because Latin was considered God's language and only the priests were allowed to interpret it. The Wycliffe Bible was the first English Bible. Copies had to be hand-written (because printing had not been invented).

Caxton invented the printing press in 1494 and turned out multiple copies of the Bible, which soon became more widely available. Within 200 years the translation band-wagon had begun to roll as reformers like Luther and Calvin taught that people should be able to read God's word for themselves. Luther began a translation into German in 1521, and several people worked on translations into English.

Tyndale's version of the New Testament in 1526 was influential and based on the original manuscripts (not translated from the Vulgate). It became the basis of all English versions to follow. Tyndale had to write it in exile and was burned at the stake for heresy. It was soon followed by Coverdale's version in 1535, the first complete English version.

The division of the Bible into verses was done by Robert Stephanus in 1551.

The Authorized (King James) version, 1611, was translated by a committee and was the most important version for the next 300 years (and still believed by some today to be in God's second language, Elizabethan English). A Revised Version was written in 1881.

During the Twentieth Century many new versions have appeared, as people have tried to keep pace with changes in our modern language. The Revised Standard Version appeared in 1952. The Roman Catholics produced their Jerusalem Bible in 1966 (revised 1985). Other popular versions include the New English Bible (1961) and Good News Bible (NT 1966 OT 1976). *The most commonly used Bible* today is probably the New International Version (NT 1973, OT 1978).

20TH CENTURY VERSIONS

American Standard Version 1901 (based on AV)
Revised Standard Version (RSV) 1952 (American)
Amplified Bible 1958
New English Bible 1961
New American Standard 1963
Jerusalem Bible 1966 – Roman Catholic
New American Bible 1970 – Roman Catholic
Good News Bible 1976
New International Version 1978
Contemporary English Version 1995

SOME INDIVIDUAL PARAPHRASES
James Moffatt – 1924
Roald Knox – 1949
JB Phillips – 1958
Kenneth Taylor, The Living Bible – 1971

There are numerous Bible paraphrases and basic-vocabulary versions, and a thousand and one different bindings with extra 'helps'. You pays your money and takes your choice, but if you get round to reading it, do yourself a favour. Ask God, who inspired it, to make it clear to you. If you do, he will begin to unlock its inner message to you – a message that lasts a lifetime.